THE
NOAH'S ARK
JOKE BOOK

Olive Branch

THE NOAH'S ARK JOKE BOOK

Olive Branch

Illustrated by Jerry Swoffs

Hippo Books
Scholastic Publications Limited
London

Scholastic Publications Ltd.,
10 Earlham Street, London WC2H 9RX, UK

Scholastic Inc.,
730 Broadway, New York, NY 10003, USA

Scholastic Tab Publications Ltd.,
123 Newkirk Road, Richmond Hill,
Ontario L4C 3G5, Canada

Ashton Scholastic Pty. Ltd.,
P O Box 579, Gosford, New South Wales,
Australia

Ashton Scholastic Ltd.,
165 Marua Road, Panmure, Auckland 6,
New Zealand

First published by
Scholastic Publications Limited, 1989

ISBN 0 590 76096 3

Made and printed by Cox and Wyman Ltd.,
Reading, Berks.

Typeset in Plantin by COLLAGE (Design in Print),
Longfield Hill, Kent.

CONTENTS

Once upon a time, according to the story in the Bible, there lived a good old man called Noah who had three sons called Shem, Ham and Japheth. They lived at a time when the world was a very violent and wicked place. One day God looked down from heaven at all the terrible things happening on earth and decided He was going to have to do something about it.

He thought about it for some time, and decided that the best thing to do would be to wipe out all the living creatures on earth — not just the bad men but *all* men, and all the animals, too. In fact, He was just about to do it when he took a last look at the earth and saw good old Noah and his sons. I've got a better idea . . . thought God.

Noah was pottering about at home one day when he heard God's voice telling him he had to build a huge boat, which in those days was called an ark, made of wood. God told him exactly how big it had to be, and that it needed three storeys, and the door should be built in the side.

"It's very important that you do this," said God, "because I'm going to send a great flood to cover the whole world, and everyone and everything is going to die — everything except you and your family and two of every living creature on earth. It's up to you, Noah, to gather all these animals together and collect enough food so that none of them starves. And you and your wife and your three sons and their wives should all get into the Ark with the animals, and that way you'll be saved."

"Well I never!" said Mrs Noah when she heard this. "Are you certain it was the word of God — or have you been drinking again, Noah?"

"I'm absolutely certain," said Noah. "If we don't build that Ark and get all the animals into it, we'll be drowned."

So from that day onwards, Noah and his three sons stopped the work they normally did and began to build the huge Ark in their back garden. And as you can imagine, all the neighbours thought they had gone quite mad!

Once the Ark was finished, Shem, Ham and Japheth travelled all over the world to collect pairs of animals, one male and one female, to go inside it. "Two camels," said Mrs Noah, ticking them off her list as they arrived. "Two wombats, two alligators — hey, Shem, you keep an eye on those alligators! Two turtles, two pigeons, two seagulls, two grass snakes, two koala bears . . . "

"Where are the ostriches?" asked Noah. "Oh dear," said Shem. "We forgot them." And off he had to go to get them. "Where are the unicorns and dragons?"

ОБНS 1 00 000

asked Noah when they got back.

"We've been looking," said Ham, "but we can't find any anywhere."

Noah shook his head and sighed. But then he felt a drop of rain and he looked up at the sky.

"Well, lads," he said. "It's too late to worry about them now. The great storm is about to begin. Let's get everything into the Ark." And so they did. It took almost a day to push all the animals up the gangplank and into their cages and pens, and to stow away all the food they'd need while they were at sea, but eventually they finished. Mrs Noah and the three wives moved all their furniture into the Ark's cabins and cooked dinner in the galley, and the eight members of the Noah family stood on the deck that night and watched the rain coming down harder and harder.

By now the neighbours had stopped laughing. The water was so deep it was flooding their homes. They came racing round to the Noahs', saying, "Have you got room for a few more on board?" but Noah just shook his head. It rained the next day, and the next, and the next, and soon the surface of the earth was covered with water. And one night, while everyone was asleep and the animals were dozing peacefully in their pens, there was a great shudder throughout the Ark and the giant ship lifted off the ground and began to float away.

Still it didn't stop raining. For forty days it kept pouring, and soon the only thing that could be seen on the water was the Ark. Even the mountains were covered with water. And, as you can imagine, everything that had been left on the surface of the earth was drowned — all the people and all the animals, and only the fish and the whales and the sharks and the other things that lived in the sea were safe.

After one hundred and fifty days God decided that that was enough, so he stopped the rain and allowed the water to begin to drain away. Japheth was keeping watch one day when he noticed that the sea seemed to be going down.

"Look, Dad," he said excitedly, "the water is getting shallower." And so it was. Soon there was a loud grinding sound.

"My goodness!" cried Japheth, looking over the side, "we've run aground!"

And so they had — right on top of Mount Ararat, which was hidden a few metres below the surface of the water. Slowly, slowly, the water went down, but it still wasn't possible to see any green land and Noah didn't want to let the animals out unless they had grass to eat and places to live. One day he had an idea. He took a white dove and let it go through the window of the Ark and the bird flew off into the distance. Round and round it went — but there was no dry patch on which it could land so it returned, tired, to the Ark.

"Oh dear," said Noah. 'What are we going to do? We're running out of food . . . "

A week later he tried again. The dove fluttered out of the window and flew away. That evening Noah was standing on the deck, puffing at his pipe (because Mrs Noah didn't allow any smoking indoors), when there was a fluttering of wings and the dove came and landed right on his shoulder. In

her beak she held a green twig and from its leaves Noah knew that it had come from an olive tree.

"Look, everyone!" he yelled. "An olive branch! The water has gone and trees are growing again! It's safe to let the animals out now."

The very next day they lowered the gangplank and the animals filed off the Ark, two by two. "It's up to you to go forth and multiply," said Noah to each of them. And in fact there were already more than two of some breeds of animal, particularly the rabbits, who had had dozens of baby rabbits while they'd been at sea! When all the animals had gone the Noah family packed up their furniture and belongings and left the Ark too, and they built themselves new houses and Shem and Ham and Japheth and their wives had lots of children, so that soon there would be plenty of people on the earth again — only this time they would be good people.

When God saw this he was pleased with Noah. "Well done!" he said. "I trusted you to build the Ark and save your family and the animals, and you did it even though everyone thought you were mad. As a token of the trust between us, I'm going to create a sign." And high in the sky God made a beautiful rainbow, which sparkled with colour.

"There!" he said. "In future, whenever it rains, there will be a rainbow to remind everyone of Noah and his Ark."

Well, that's the story of Noah's Ark, more or less as it's told in the Bible. But I'd like to think that while they were bobbing around on the ocean with a boat full of wild animals, the Noahs had a good time. What the Bible doesn't tell us is that Shem did most of the cooking on board, though he was a terrible cook, and Ham and Noah did all the painting and repairs required to keep the Ark watertight. Japheth looked after the animals and was kept busy feeding and watering them all, and Mrs Noah not only did the housework but she also cared for any animals who were sick or unhappy. They had a terrific time together, and to keep cheerful they told each other jokes. They even found time to put together this brilliant joke book, which, as you'll see for yourself, is all about life aboard the Ark. Enjoy it — and remember, next time you see a rainbow think of good old Noah and his family all at sea!

ARK AT THIS!

Here are six jokes that Noah wrote when he was aboard the Ark:

What was Noah's job?
He was an Ark-itect.

Why couldn't Shem, Ham and Japheth play cards on Noah's Ark?
Because Noah always stood on the deck.

Was it dark on Noah's Ark at night?
No, because Noah installed flood lighting!

What's the difference between Noah's Ark and Joan of Arc?
The first was made of wood and the second was Maid of Orleans.

Where did Noah keep his bees?
In the Ark-hives.

Was Noah keen on bottling fruit?
No, but he was good at preserving pairs.

THE ELEPHANTS ARE COMING!

Let's start with the biggest jokers of all — the elephants!

Which creatures took the most luggage into the Ark?
The elephants – they had two trunks.

SHEM: Have one of these buns.
MRS NOAH: No thanks, they're too fattening.
SHEM: Fattening?
MRS NOAH: Have you seen the size of those elephants?

14

What's the difference between a flea and an elephant?
An elephant can have fleas but a flea can't have elephants.

HAM: I'd like an elephant sandwich for lunch please.
SHEM: How do I make an elephant sandwich?
HAM: You start with a massive loaf . . .

What does Mrs Noah do with a blue elephant?
She tells it a joke and cheers it up.

EDWARD ELEPHANT: I'm drunk!
EDNA ELEPHANT: How can you be sure?
EDWARD ELEPHANT: I keep seeing pink people floating in front of my eyes.

What happened when the mad professor crossed an elephant with a computer?
He came up with the biggest know-all in the world.

MRS NOAH: What should you give a seasick elephant?
NOAH: Plenty of room.

What's grey and wrinkly and lights up in the dark?
An electric elephant.

MRS NOAH: I wonder what we'd get if we crossed an elephant with some peanut butter?
NOAH: Either an elephant that sticks to the roof of your mouth, or peanut butter that never forgets.

NOAH: Will the elephants eat the penguins?
JAPHETH: No, they can't get the wrappers off . . .

What is huge, green and has a trunk?
An unripe elephant.

MRS NOAH: What are we going to do if one of the elephants charges?
NOAH: Pay him!

What do you get when you cross an elephant and a butterfly?
A mam-moth.

NOAH: What's the difference between an elephant and a matterdear?
MRS NOAH: What's a matterdear?
NOAH: Nothing much, darling.

What's the same size as an elephant but weighs nothing at all?
An elephant's shadow.

EDWARD ELEPHANT: Why are you painting the soles of your feet yellow?
EDNA ELEPHANT: So that I can hide upside down in Shem's custard.
EDWARD ELEPHANT: I've never seen you hide in the custard.
EDNA ELEPHANT: See, it works!

Why do elephants wear green felt hats?
So they can walk across snooker tables without being seen.

HAM: This elephant is very nervous!
JAPHETH: I'll give him some trunkquillizers.

What's red outside, grey inside and very, very crowded?
A London bus full of elephants.

NOAH: Where can you buy really ancient elephants?
SHEM: I've no idea.
NOAH: At a mammoth spring sale.

What game do elephants play in the back seat of a car?
Squash.

EDNA ELEPHANT: Why have you painted yourself all the colours of the rainbow?
EDWARD ELEPHANT: I thought I'd hide in the paintbox.

How can you tell when there's an elephant hiding under your bed?
Because your nose touches the ceiling.

SHEM: What's the difference between an African and an Indian elephant?
JAPHETH: About 3,200 miles.

What's the best way to stop an elephant charging?
Take away his American Express card.

MRS NOAH: How can you tell when there's an elephant in your gravy?
HAM: When it's very, very lumpy.

Why do African elephants have big ears?
Because Noddy won't pay the ranson.

HAM: Can I have an elephant sandwich for lunch?

SHEM: Sorry, but I can't do an elephant sandwich.
HAM: Why not?
SHEM: We've run out of bread.

Why did the elephant tie a knot in his trunk?
So he wouldn't forget.

SHEM: One of the elephants has been in the fridge!
NOAH: How can you tell?
SHEM: He's left footprints in the butter.

How do you get an elephant into a matchbox?
First you take out all the matches . . .

JAPHETH: How do you get down from an elephant?
NOAH: You don't get down from an elephant — you get down from a duck.

NOAH: What's the difference between an elephant and a chocolate digestive biscuit?
HAM: You can't dip an elephant in your tea.

Why was the fat elephant frightened of going to sea in the Ark?
He was a non-slimmer.

MRS NOAH: Why are elephants so big and grey and wrinkly?
NOAH: Because if they were small and round and red they'd be Smarties.

Why can't Edna and Edward go swimming at the same time?
Because they've only got one pair of trunks between them.

EDNA ELEPHANT: I once worked in a circus.
EDWARD ELEPHANT: Why did you leave?
EDNA ELEPHANT: I got fed up working for peanuts.

What was an elephant doing on the M25?
About ten miles an hour.

JAPHETH: What's the difference between a flea, an elephant and a pot of glue?
HAM: I don't know. What *is* the difference between a flea, an elephant and a pot of glue?
JAPHETH: An elephant can have fleas but a flea can't have elephants.
HAM: And what about the pot of glue?
JAPHETH: I knew you'd get stuck there.

What time is it when the elephant sits on the lifeboat?
Time to get a new lifeboat.

What did the hotel manager say to the elephant who couldn't pay his bill?
"Just pack your trunk and get out of here!"

SHEM: What's the difference between a cherry and a white elephant?
MRS NOAH: The cherry is red.

What does Noah say when he has to tell the elephants off?
Tusk, tusk!

MRS NOAH: Help! Help! One of the elephants has broken its toe!
NOAH: We'd better send for the tow truck.

How can you tell if an elephant has been in your bed?
Because of the peanut shells it leaves behind.

JAPHETH: Dad, do you think it's possible for a man to fall in love with an elephant?

NOAH: No, son, it's out of the question.

JAPHETH: In that case, do you know anyone who'd like to buy a very big engagement ring?

NOAH: I wonder why the elephants are so wrinkled?

JAPHETH: Have you ever tried to iron one?

HAM: I think Edward the elephant has been sleeping in my bed!

MRS NOAH: How do you know?

HAM: Because under the pillow I found a huge pair of pyjamas with the letter E on the pocket.

SHEM: Is there anything worse than a giraffe with a sore throat?
JAPHETH: An elephant with a cold in the nose.

What do elephants have that no other animal has?
Baby elephants.

EDWARD ELEPHANT: I wonder why I'm so big and strong and you're so tiny and weak?
MICHAEL MOUSE: Well, I wasn't very well last week.

Why is Edward wearing soft-soled shoes?
So he can creep up behind mice and surprise them.

NOAH: I'd like to put an advert in the newspaper.
NEWSPAPER MAN: A small ad, sir?
NOAH: No, a big ad. I want to sell an elephant.

How do elephants get down from trees?
They stand on a leaf and wait for autumn to come.

EDWARD ELEPHANT: Why are you painting your toenails red?
EDNA ELEPHANT: So I can hide up a cherry tree.

Why do elephants have trunks?
Because they can't carry suitcases.

MRS NOAH: Why do those elephants drink so much water?
JAPHETH: Because no one offers them anything else.

How do you stop an elephant getting through the eye of a needle?
Just tie a knot in its tail.

MRS NOAH: What's the best way to tell the difference between an elephant and a box of chocolates?
SHEM: Lift it up. If you can't it's either an elephant or the biggest box of chocolates in the world.

How can you tell an elephant from a mouse?
A mouse never remembers.

EDWARD ELEPHANT: Why are you painting your head yellow?
EDNA ELEPHANT: I heard that blondes have more fun and I thought I'd try it out.

Why are elephants such terrible dancers?
They have two left feet.

JAPHETH: I wonder what would happen if I crossed one of the elephants with one of the whales?
SHEM: You'd get a huge pair of swimming trunks.

Is it very difficult to bury a dead elephant?
Yes, it's a huge undertaking.

JAPHETH: I'm so strong I could lift an elephant with one hand.
NOAH: But where are you going to find an elephant with one hand?

What's the difference between an elephant and a banana?
Have you tried peeling an elephant?

NOAH: What's the difference between an elephant and a packet of cornflakes?
SHEM: I don't know.
NOAH: In that case I'm never going to send you out to buy the cornflakes!

Why did the elephant cross the road?
Because it was the chicken's day off.

NOAH: I wonder what we'd get if we crossed Edna with a kangaroo?
HAM: Huge holes all over the Ark?

What's pink and grey, pink and grey, pink and grey . . . ?
Edna rolling down a hill.

Edna the elephant was getting too fat. "Now look, Edna," said Japheth, "you can have ten apples, a lettuce and half a gallon of orange juice a day. That should make you lose weight."

"Yummy," said Edna. "Do I eat that before or after meals?"

SHEM: Are elephants found at the North Pole?
JAPHETH: No, elephants are so big they never get lost.

How do you get four elephants in a Mini?
Two in the back and two in the front.

HAM: When an elephant squirts water from its trunk, is it very powerful?
JAPHETH: I'll say — a jumbo jet can fly 400 people across the Atlantic!

What's yellow outside, grey inside, and never forgets?
An elephant omelette

How much did the psychiatrist charge the elephant?
Twenty pounds for the visit and two hundred pounds for a new couch.

EDNA ELEPHANT: I can jump higher than a lamp-post.
EDWARD ELEPHANT: No you can't.
EDNA ELEPHANT: Have you ever seen a lamp-post jump?

What happens when an elephant sits in front of the television set?
You miss most of the programme.

MRS NOAH: How would an elephant smell without his trunk?
JAPHETH: He'd still smell pretty terrible!

NOAH: Have you ever wondered why elephants are grey?
JAPHETH: So that you can tell them apart from canaries, I suppose.

What do you call an elephant wearing ear plugs?
Anything you want because he can't hear.

What's grey and red all over?
A sunburned elephant.

JAPHETH: Help! Edward has just swallowed a bullet!
HAM: Well, don't point his trunk at me!

What did Noah say when he saw the elephants coming towards him?
"Look out, here come the elephants!"
What did Noah say when he saw the elephants coming towards him with sunglasses on?
Nothing, because he didn't recognize them.

SHEM: Why do elephants have bulgy ankles?
JAPHETH: Because their socks are too tight.

SHEM: I think there's an elephant in the oven.
MRS NOAH: How can you tell?
SHEM: I can't shut the door.

Why can't elephants fly on planes?
Because their trunks won't fit under the seats.

Why did Edna wear training shoes?
Because her high heels were at the shoemenders.

Why did Edna and Edward wear dark glasses?
Because if you'd had this many stupid jokes told about you, you wouldn't want anyone to recognize you either!

BEASTLY GIGGLES

MRS NOAH: What's that terrible noise?
NOAH: It's just the cows.
MRS NOAH: But what are they doing?
NOAH: They're playing moo-sical chairs.

What instrument does the fish play in the Ark pop group?
The bass guitar.

MRS NOAH: Can we get some Swedish cattle for the Ark?
NOAH: No, the Swedes like to keep their Stockholm.

Which is the only animal on the Ark to wear a toupee?
The ear-wig.

NOAH: The chickens want to play football.
JAPHETH: Why?
NOAH: Because there are ducks in cricket.

NOAH: Where have you been?
SHEM: The sheepdog trials.
NOAH: What happened?
SHEM: They were all found not guilty.

NOAH: Did you go the wolves' party?
SHEM: Yes.
NOAH: Enjoy yourself?
SHEM: Yes, it was a howling success.

What dance do ducks prefer?
The quackstep.

NOAH: I'm awfully sorry, but I've just run over your cat. I'd like to replace it.
JAPHETH: All right — are you any good at catching mice?

Where do bees go to catch transport?
The buzz-stop.

SHEM: This pig is sick.
MRS NOAH: Well, call for a hambulance.

What did the sardines say when they saw a submarine go by?
"There goes a can of people."

NOAH: I've got a new hobby.
JAPHETH: What is it?
NOAH: Racing pigeons.
JAPHETH: And do you ever beat them?

Did you hear what happened during the milking contest on the Ark? There was udder chaos.

MRS NOAH: I think I'll take up swimming. They say it keeps your figure trim.
JAPHETH: Don't do it, Mum.
MRS NOAH: Why not?
JAPHETH: Haven't you ever seen a whale?

MRS NOAH: Why is this glow-worm so sad?
NOAH: Because she doesn't know if she's coming or glowing.

A family went out one day and bought a kitten. They came home and put it on a cushion in front of the fire to keep warm. Later, little Kevin went to have a look at it and found that the kitten was purring. "Mum, come quick!" he called, "The kitten's coming to the boil!"

Why are worms like naughty children?
Because they both wriggle out of things.

What did the buffalo say when his little boy went to school?
"Bison!"

NOAH: Why are you riding that horse?
JAPHETH: Because it's too heavy to carry.

What's the best way of stopping a dog barking in the hold of the Ark?
Put him on the deck of the Ark.

MRS NOAH: This chicken's been drinking whisky!
HAM: How can you tell?
MRS NOAH: It's laying Scotch eggs.

What do pigs use to write letters?
A pen and oink.

SHEM: I've just crossed a cow, a sheep and a baby goat.
HAM: And what did you get?
SHEM: A Milky Baa Kid.

How do bugs wheel their children around?
In baby buggies.

Two seagulls were flying over the white cliffs of Dover when Concorde came past. "Wow!" said one. "I wish I could fly that fast."

"You could," said the other, "if your tail was on fire."

HAM: Have you ever seen a man-eating shark?
JAPHETH: No, but I once saw a man eating cod at the fish and chip shop.

NOAH: Why does that boxer dog have such an ugly flat face?
HAM: He used to chase parked cars.

JAPHETH: It's time for these tadpoles to become frogs.
MRS NOAH: They'd better go to the croakroom while they change.

MRS NOAH: It's raining cats and dogs out there.
NOAH: I know — I just stepped in a poodle.

When is it bad luck to have a black cat cross your path?
When you're a mouse.

NOAH: What's a buttress?
MRS NOAH: A lady goat?

Why was the crab arrested?
Because it kept pinching things.

What is a camel?
A horse designed by a committee.

JAPHETH: The kangaroos have just decided to get married.
MRS NOAH: How romantic!
JAPHETH: Let's hope they live hoppily ever after.

Why is a horse just like a cricket match?
Because they both get stopped by the rein.

SHEM: I ate an electric eel the other day.
MRS NOAH: What on earth did it taste like?
SHEM: Shocking!

What's black and white and can't sit down?
A skunk with nappy rash.

NOAH: Did you hear what happened to the flea circus?
SHEM: No, what happened?
NOAH: A dog came by and stole the show.

What does a camel become after it's one year old?
Two years old.

Why did the bus stop?
Because it saw the zebra crossing.

MRS NOAH: This cat is very clever.
NOAH: Why, what does it do?
MRS NOAH: It eats some cheese, then breathes down the mouseholes.

What do you get if you cross a wild dog with the Beatles' drummer?
Dingo Starr.

What's green and terribly dangerous?
A caterpillar with a machine gun.

MRS NOAH: I think that cow over there is my favourite. She's such a lovely colour.
NOAH: It's a Jersey.
MRS NOAH: Oh, I thought it was the colour of her skin.

Which animal's eye makes a good target?
A bull's eye.

MRS NOAH: That cat's just swallowed a duck!
NOAH: Does that make it a duck-filled fatty puss?

SHEM: Sometimes I wonder why this old Ark doesn't fall apart.
JAPHETH: It's because the woodworm are holding hands.

What did one mother kangaroo say to the other mother kangaroo?
"I hate rainy days when the children have to play inside!"

JAPHETH: I've just crossed a panda with a harmonium.
NOAH: And what did you get?
JAPHETH: A pandemonium.

What did Shem say when he saw a snake for the first time?
"Oh, look! Here's a tail without a head!"

Mrs Noah went to her local hardware shop. "Do you have any rat poison?" she asked.

"Have you tried Boots?" replied the assistant.

"I want to poison them," grumbled Mrs Noah, "not kick them to death."

How can you get eggs without keeping hens?
By keeping ducks instead.

SHEM: I used to be my teacher's pet.
HAM: That must have been nice.
SHEM: Not really — she would have preferred a cat.

JAPHETH: I've had to put the gnus in two separate enclosures.
NOAH: Why is that?
JAPHETH: Because there's good gnus and bad gnus.

Why did the cow sit on the spin dryer?
Because she wanted to make milk shake.

NOAH: How did you break your leg?
SHEM: Do you see those steps down to the bottom deck?
NOAH: Yes.
SHEM: Well, I didn't.

What came out of the wardrobe at one hundred miles an hour?
Stirling Moth.

NOAH: The horses want to go to the theatre.
JAPHETH: Okay, let's book them stalls for Friday night.

What do cows like doing on a Saturday night?
Going to the moo-vies.

NOAH: Someone's been stealing our cattle!
SHEM: It must be a beefburglar.

JAPHETH: Come quick! The pig's ill!
MRS NOAH: Poor thing, he's got a sore throat.
JAPHETH: What he needs is some oinkment!

What do you call a sick reptile?
An illigator.

HAM: Here's a problem for you to solve. A horse wanted to cross the river to get to a field with lots of lovely grass, but there was no bridge, no ferry and the river was too wide to swim. How did the horse get across?
NOAH: I give up.
HAM: So did the horse.

What does a Hindu?
It lays eggs.

SHEM: We've got to do something to stop the moles digging holes all over the Ark.
NOAH: Let's confiscate their spades.

NOAH: Which two fish do you need to make a shoe?

HAM: I don't know.

NOAH: A sole and an eel.

What happened to Ray when Edna the elephant sat on him?

He became an X-ray.

SHEM: How do you spell rhinoceros?

JAPHETH: R-I-N-O-C-E-R-O-S.

SHEM: In the dictionary it's spelled R-H-I-N-O-C-E-R-O-S.

JAPHETH: You didn't ask me how the dictionary spells it.

RALPH RHINO: What's that thing over there?

ROBERTA RHINO: It's a hippopotamus.

RALPH RHINO: Poor thing — fancy having such an ugly face!

What do you get if you cross a giant gorilla with a skunk?

King Pong.

NOAH: Those sheep need a haircut.

JAPHETH: Can you trim them?

NOAH: No, they'll have to go to the baa-baa's shop.

A mother lion stood and watched as her young son chased a hunter round and round a tree. "Stop doing that!" she scolded him. "Haven't I told you a hundred times not to play with your food?"

Why is a leopard in the desert like Father Christmas?
Because it has Sandy Claws.

Japheth was bitten by one of the dogs and went to see the doctor. "I'm terribly sorry," said the doctor, "but it looks as if you have rabies — and it's likely to be fatal."

"In that case," said Japheth, "please pass me that sheet of paper and a pencil".

"Are you going to make your will?" asked the doctor.

"No, I'm going to make a list of people I want to bite."

Where did knights of old park their camels?
Camelot.

NOAH: Something's been puzzling me. Why do cows have horns?
MRS NOAH: In case their bells don't work, stupid!

Are dinosaurs good at passing exams?
Yes, they do so with extinction.

NOAH: Why is that glow-worm crying?
MRS NOAH: Poor thing — he's got glowing pains.

Mrs Noah was out shopping for fruit and vegetables one day when she spotted some lovely tomatoes. "They're beautiful," she said.

"They are, aren't they?" said the greengrocer. "They're from the Canaries."

"How strange," said Mrs Noah. "I always thought they were grown on plants, not laid."

HAM: Why do they say that dolphins are so incredibly intelligent?

NOAH: Just think about it. Within weeks of captivity they've trained a man to stand on the side of their pool and throw them fish three times a day.

Which is the only house in which it's impossible for a mouse to live?
A snail's house.

Ham came storming into his father's office and flung down an envelope on the table. "After all the work I do on this Ark!" he yelled. "I'm busy all hours of the day and night, and you give me this poultry pay-cheque!"

"You mean paltry," said Noah.

"No I don't," said Ham. "This is chicken feed!"

SHEM: That dog's eating my book!

MRS NOAH: Well, don't just shout — take the words right out of his mouth!

Noah came into the cabin one evening looking worried. "I've just realized that we don't have any licences for the dogs on board the Ark," he said.

"Don't be silly, dear," said Mrs Noah. "None of the dogs can drive!"

NOAH: I see the squirrels are playing football this afternoon.

HAM: What's the team called?

NOAH: Nuts Forest.

NOAH: I think that frog is a spy.
MRS NOAH: You mean he's a croak and dagger agent?

What did the mouse say when it broke two teeth?
Hard cheese!

Japheth went to the pet shop. "I'd like some bird seed, please," he said.

"How many birds have you got to feed?" asked the assistant.

"None," said Japheth. "I want to grow some."

What exams are horses good at?
Hay levels.

Mrs Noah went to buy a new winter coat and tried on a red one made of pure wool. "Can this wool coat be worn in the rain?" she asked.

"Of course, madam," said the assistant. "When did you last see a sheep carrying an umbrella?"

What happened when the letter M got into the fridge?
It turned the ice into mice.

NOAH: What's the difference between a flea and a coyote?
JAPHETH: I've no idea.
NOAH: One howls on the prairie and the other prowls on the hairy.

Which ducks go "bang" on Bonfire night?
Firequackers.

NOAH: That clock is completely crazy.
SHEM: Why do you say that?
NOAH: It's a cuckoo clock.

MRS NOAH: That chicken keeps using fowl language!
SHEM: If she doesn't behave better, we'll have her eggsterminated!

NOAH: One of the skunks has died of 'flu.
MRS NOAH: I didn't know skunks could catch 'flu.
NOAH: This one *flew* across the deck and over the side of the Ark.

NOAH: What's wrong with you?
HAM: I just walked under a cow.
NOAH: So what?
HAM: I got a pat on the head.

What leaves yellow footprints on the seabed?
A lemon sole.

JAPHETH: I've just crossed a carpet with a hippopotamus.
MRS NOAH: And what did you get?
JAPHETH: A huge pile on the sitting-room floor.

NOAH: Why is that hen sitting on your head?
SHEM: I heard that egg shampoo was good for your hair.

Which animal always drives down the centre lane of the motorway?
A road hog.

JAPHETH: I'm starving — I haven't had a square meal all day!
MRS NOAH: You poor thing. Have a dog biscuit.

SHEM: I've just seen a prehistoric cow.
NOAH: Where did you see it?
SHEM: In the moo-seum.

Why are goldfish red?
The water makes them rusty.

MRS NOAH: I think the black chickens must be more intelligent than the white chickens.
NOAH: Why do you say that?
MRS NOAH: Well, the black hens can lay white eggs but the white hens can't lay black eggs.

What is the communist cat's favourite book?
The Thoughts of Chairman Miaow.

FIRST CHICKEN: I've just laid an egg six centimetres long. No one can beat that!
SECOND CHICKEN: Mrs Noah can.
FIRST CHICKEN: How?
SECOND CHICKEN: With an egg beater!

When the baby bear was born, who came to write about the story for the local paper?
The cub reporter.

Why do pandas eat bamboo shoots?
Because no one gives them anything else.

MRS NOAH: Help! The baby goat fell into the food processor!
HAM: What happened?
MRS NOAH: It's now a crazy mixed up kid . . .

What coat has the most sleeves?
A coat of arms for an octopus.

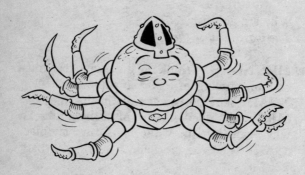

MRS NOAH: Does this dog like children?
SHEM: Yes, but he prefers Pedigree Chum and Winalot.

Why did the dog keep howling?
Because he was barking up the wrong tree.

NOAH: I think we'll call that cockerel Robinson.
MRS NOAH: Why's that?
NOAH: Because he Crusoe loudly last night.

Why did the chicken board the Ark?
To escape from Colonel Sanders.

SHEM: There's a dead beetle in this soup.
HAM: No wonder — they're lousy swimmers.

NOAH: Send the chicken on to the football pitch.
HAM: But why?
NOAH: Because the referee just whistled for a fowl.

NOAH: I used to have a parrot. I had it for five years and in all that time it never said a word.
HAM: Maybe it was tongue tied.
NOAH: No, it was stuffed.

MRS NOAH: What do you call that baby whale?
NOAH: A little squirt.

MRS NOAH: I made a chicken pie but the dog's eaten it!
NOAH: Never mind — we can always get another dog.

What do frogs like to drink?
Croaka-cola.

NOAH: The skunks want a chemistry set for Christmas.
MRS NOAH: I don't think that's a good idea.
NOAH: Why not?
MRS NOAH: They might smell the Ark out.

MRS NOAH: There's something wrong with that cow.
JAPHETH: She looks all right to me.
MRS NOAH: No, she's moo-dy.

How can you tell a baby snake?
By its rattle.

What did the grizzly bear say when he saw Santa Claus?
Yum, yum!

SHEM: I just crossed a police inspector with an octopus.
MRS NOAH: And what did you get?
SHEM: A policeman with eight long arms of the law.

NOAH: The chickens are having a trial.
JAPHETH: Why?
NOAH: One of them has committed murder.
JAPHETH: And what was the jury's verdict?
NOAH: Guilty, so now the villain will be eggsecuted.

What happened when Mrs Noah kissed one of the toads at a party?
She turned into a frog.

NOAH: I've just crossed a cow with a mule.
MRS NOAH: And what have you got?
NOAH: Milk with a real kick in it.

The mother rabbit was having trouble with her children who all kept asking where they had come from. "I'm far too busy to answer that question," said Mother rabbit.

"*Please*, Mum!" said all the rabbits. "Tell us!"

"All right," said Mother rabbit. "If you really want to know, you were all pulled out of a magican's hat."

What are secret agents' favourite creatures?
Spy-ders.

NOAH: I'm going to call that horse Fireplace.
MRS NOAH: Why is that?
NOAH: Because it has a blaze on its forehead.

What do you call a laid-back, long-haired, half-ton animal?
A hippie-potamus.

How do you spell mousetrap in just three letters?
C-A-T.

What happened when Mrs Noah built an ant hill in her window box?
She had ants in her plants.

NOAH: Why is that cat called Carpenter?
MRS NOAH: He keeps doing little jobs around the house.

MRS NOAH: Have you seen the turtle who always dresses fashionably?
JAPHETH: No, what does he wear?
MRS NOAH: A people-necked sweater.

Why did the spider get angry with the beetle?
Because he kept bugging him.

SHEM: I wish I had the money to buy a pedigree Arab horse.
MRS NOAH: What on earth do you want to buy an Arab horse for?
SHEM: I don't — I just wish I had that much money.

NOAH: Those American stoats want to get married.

MRS NOAH: Then they'll be the United Stoats of America!

Why did Little Bo Peep lose her sheep?
Because she had a crook with her.

JAPHETH: Did you hear the joke about the eight stupid monkeys called Do, Re, Fa, Sol, La, Ti and Do?

HAM: What about Mi?

JAPHETH: Whoops! I'd forgotten about you.

Why wouldn't the hen get into a fight?
Because she was chicken.

SHEM: It's impossible to have a conversation with all these goats around.

JAPHETH: Why?

SHEM: Because they keep butting in!

What wears a fur coat all winter and pants in the summer?
A dog.

MRS NOAH: This is very strange — I can't get these tiles to stick to the bathroom wall.
JAPHETH: You're not supposed to use reptiles!

SHEM: That dog has a very strange bark.
MRS NOAH: That's because he's a Pekinese and he barks with a Chinese accent.

What kind of tie do pigs wear?
Pigsties.

JAPHETH: I gave that cow a five pound note to eat.

NOAH: Why on earth did you do that?

JAPHETH: To see if it makes her milk richer.

MRS NOAH: Help! A bird just flew off with my purse!

SHEM: Bet it was a robin.

A guide was taking a hunter on an African safari. They were hiding in a tree when a leopard came into view. "Go on, shoot it on the spot!" said the guide.

"Could you be more precise and tell me *which* spot?" asked the hunter.

NOAH: What are all those cows doing round the TV set?

JAPHETH: They're watching their favourite TV programme.

NOAH: Oh, *Dr Moo!*

"Come and look at what I've done!" called Ham, and everyone came to look out of the porthole where a rope was hanging.

"Very nice, dear," said Mrs Noah. "What's it for?"

"It's my weather forecaster," said Ham.

"But how does it work?" asked Noah.

"Well," said Ham, "when it moves, it's windy out there, and when it's wet, it's raining."

Who eats its victims two by two?
Noah's Shark!

JAPHETH: You should never tell your secrets to the pigs.
SHEM: Why not?
JAPHETH: Because they're all squealers.

MONKEYING AROUND

Of all the animals on the Ark, the monkeys are the naughtiest. They swing from the mast and turn somersaults round the TV aerials — and on Mondays they even steal Mrs Noah's washing from the washing-line! Here are a few of their favourite jokes . . .

MRS NOAH: This monkey's like a flower.
NOAH: What kind of flower?
MRS NOAH: A chimp-pansy.

What do you do if a gorilla decides to sleep in your bed?
You sleep somewhere else!

JAPHETH: Do you know what it means when a gorilla bangs his chest?
HAM: He's got indigestion?

How do the monkeys make toast on the Ark?
They put the bread under a g'rilla.

60

SHEM: Did you see how that chimp escaped from his cage?
NOAH: No.
SHEM: He used a monkey wrench.

Why do the monkeys swing from the mast?
Because there are no swings to swing from on the Ark.

Which monkey was Emperor of France?
Napoleon Baboonaparte.

What's the difference between a gorilla and a baked bean?.
A gorilla doesn't slide off the end of your fork.

What can a chimp touch with his right hand that he can't touch with his left?
His left elbow.

NOAH: Where's the best place to buy a gorilla?
SHEM: I don't know.
NOAH: At a jungle sale.

What's hairy, sticky and swings from branch to branch?
A meringue-utan.

JAPHETH: Did you hear about the monkey who ran all the way from John O'Groats to Land's End?
SHEM: No, I didn't.
JAPHETH: Neither did I!

What's the difference between a gorilla and a banana?
Have you ever seen a gorilla in a fruit bowl?

What do lady gorillas wear when they do the cleaning?
Ape-rons.

SHEM: I'd like to buy a chimpanzee, please.
SALESMAN: Yes, monkeys are fifty pounds apiece.
SHEM: I don't want pieces, I need a whole one.

SHEM: These monkeys are terrible gossips.
MRS NOAH: Yes, that one's a real *blab*-boon.

JAPHETH: It's terrible, Mum. Whenever I shut my eyes I can see huge hairy gorillas.
MRS NOAH: Have you ever seen a psychiatrist?
JAPHETH: No, just these huge hairy gorillas.

Did you hear about the stupid gorilla who had a flea in his ear? He shot it.

MRS NOAH: That chimp is looking very pleased with himself!

HAM: Yes, his sister has just had a baby.

MRS NOAH: I see — so he's a monkey's uncle!

What happened when the monkey fell out of the tree and into the sea?
It was just a drop in the ocean.

Did you hear about the gorilla who got stuck in a revolving door? He didn't know if he was coming or going.

NOAH: That monkey isn't well.

SHEM: What's wrong with him?

NOAH: Ape-endicitis.

Why did the gorilla give up boxing?
He didn't want to spoil his good looks.

NOAH: I notice that chimp is wearing an army uniform.

JAPHETH: That's right — he's an expert on gorilla warfare.

CREEPY CRAWLY CORNER

Down at the bottom of the Ark, where it's dark and damp and dingy, live all the creepy crawly creatures. If you don't mind spiders and snakes and ants and worms, read on . . .

What does Mrs Noah give the ants when they are ill?
Ant-ibiotics.

HAM: What's the difference between a worm and a caterpillar?
JAPHETH: A caterpillar is a worm with a woolly jumper on.

Where do spiders play football?
At Webley.

BABY SNAKE: Are we poisonous, Mummy?
MOTHER SNAKE: Why do you ask?
BABY SNAKE: I just bit my tongue!

After the Flood was over and the water had drained away, Noah decided it was time to let all the creatures out of the Ark. He and Shem lowered the gangplank and the animals began to file down. "Remember," called Noah, "you must go forth and multiply! Goodbye, lions! Goodbye camels! Goodbye hamsters!" Off went the animals.

When they'd all gone, Noah and Shem went down to their cabin for a nice cup of tea. As they were sitting in the galley they heard a hissing noise coming from a dark corner. "What's that?" said Noah, and he went over to have a look. Hiding in the dark corner were two snakes. "What are you two doing here?" he asked. "Didn't you hear me telling everyone to go forth and multiply?"

"Yes, we did," said one of the snakes, "but we've got a problem. We can't multiply — we're adders."

HAM: I wonder where the fleas hide in winter?
JAPHETH: Search me!

What's the smallest type of ant in the world?
An infant.

How do fleas go around the Ark?
By itch-hiking.

What did the earwig say when he fell overboard?
"''Ere we go!''"

NOAH: Did you hear what happened to the stupid jellyfish?
MRS NOAH: No, what happened?
NOAH: It set!

How does Mrs Noah keep flies out of the kitchen?
She keep a bucket of elephant manure in the lounge.

MRS NOAH: Why do those ants keep running along the cereal packet?
SHEM: Because it say on the flap "Tear along the dotted line".

What did the ant say to the bee?
"Give me your honey or your life."

As well as all the animals on board the Ark, there were other living things that Noah didn't know about — including some bacteria which were living on an old piece of of cheese that Shem had thrown away in a dark corner. One morning one bacterium came across another who didn't look very well. "What's the matter with you?" he asked.

"You'd better keep away from me," said the other. "I think I've caught penicillin."

JAPHETH: My fleas are always happy.
HAM: Are they really?
JAPHETH: Yes, they're hoptimists!

HAM: Have you seen Shem's bird impressions?
NOAH: No, what does he do?
HAM: He eats worms!

HAM: Dad, what has orange and purple stripes, ten hairy green legs and two big yellow eyes sticking out on stalks?
NOAH: I've no idea. Why?
HAM: There's one crawling up your leg!

What sits on the front of the Ark going "Croak! Croak!" when it's misty?
A frog-horn.

Mrs Noah — whose first name is Emma —
Was seized by a terrible tremor.
    She had swallowed a spider
    Which stung her inside her —
Gadzooks! What an awful dilemma!

How does Noah send messages from the Ark?
He uses the Morse toad.

FELIX FLEA: I say, my dear, you're not looking too good.
FIONA FLEA: No, I'm not really up to scratch.

Where do frogs sit?
On toadstools.

NOAH: Aaaagh! Look, there's a worm on my plate!
SHEM: Don't panic — it's just a slim sausage.

What's worse than taking a bite of an apple and finding a maggot?
Taking a bite of an apple and finding half a maggot . . .

What made the caterpillar miss the Ark football match?
He was putting his boots on.

Noah was out on deck one day when he saw Japheth dangling a fishing rod over the side of the Ark. "What are you doing?" he yelled. "We've only got two maggots — you mustn't use them for fishing!"

"I'm not fishing," said Japheth, "I'm just teaching them how to swim."

What did the caterpillars do on New Year's Day?
They turned over a new leaf.

What has six legs, wears a false moustache and listens to other people's coversations?
A telephone bug.

How does Japheth tell which end of the worm is which?
He tickles it in the middle and sees which end laughs.

NOAH: What's that noise? It goes 99-thump, 99-thump . . .
JAPHETH: That's the centipede with the wooden leg.

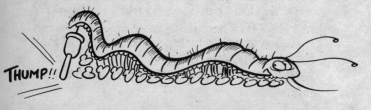

THUMP!!

What's white on the outside and green on the inside?
A frog sandwich.

What did the centipede say to his girlfriend?
"You've got a lovely pair of legs, pair of legs, pair of legs . . . "

HAM: What shall I call the two spiders now they've got married?
JAPHETH: Newly-webs?

What do you call two snakes on your car windscreen?
Windscreen vipers.

What do you call a creepy crawly from outer space?
Bug Rogers.

SHEM: What's the difference between a man who's just been bitten by a mosquito and a runner about to start a race?
HAM: I don't know.
SHEM: One man is starting to itch and the other is itching to start.

Where can you find giant snails?
At the ends of giants' fingers.

JAPHETH: These mosquitoes are making me annoyed.
SHEM: Why's that?
JAPHETH: They're really getting under my skin.

Two bluebottle flies were playing football in a saucer. One of them said to the other, "We're going to have to practise harder — we're playing in the Cup next Saturday."

What happens when a flea is furious?
It gets hopping mad.

What time is it when a flea and a fly pass by?
Fly past flea.

MRS NOAH: What's that thing, lying on the ground and 100 feet up in the air?
HAM: A centipede sunbathing.

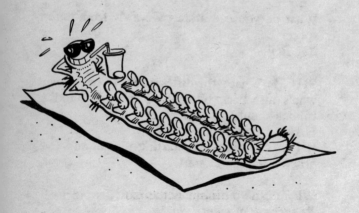

SHEM: There are two maggots here. They want to come aboard the Ark in an apple.
NOAH: Sorry, but they've got to be in pairs (pears).

What happened when the two head-lice moved into the Ark?
They held a louse-warming party.

SHEM: What are you eating?
HAM: An apple.
SHEM: Watch out for those worms!
HAM: When I eat an apple the worms have to look out for themselves.

What do you call the world's largest ant?
Gi-ant.

JAPHETH: This ant is the most stupid I've ever seen.
HAM: What's its name?
JAPHETH: Antwerp.

NOAH: The frogs want to fly their flag.
MRS NOAH: What can we fly it from?
NOAH: How about the tad-pole?

What happens to the ants when they stop running around all day?
They get stepped on at night.

JAPHETH: Help! The ants have run away to get married!
MRS NOAH: You mean they've ant-eloped?

What happened to the snake who had a cold?
She adder viper nose.

NOAH: What present can we give the spiders for Christmas?
JAPHETH: How about four pairs of socks?

How many legs does an ant have?
Two – just like an uncle.

HAM: Hey, what's this fly doing in my soup?
SHEM: It looks like the backstroke to me.

What kind of flowers do frogs like best?
Croakuses.

JAPHETH: I've been trying to play jokes on these snakes but it doesn't work.
NOAH: Why not?
JAPHETH: It's impossible to pull their legs.

Which is the bossiest ant in the Ark?
The tyrant.

MRS NOAH: Aren't the flies thick around here?
NOAH: You prefer thin ones, then, do you?

What did one caterpillar say to the other when they saw a butterfly?
You're never going to get me up in one of those things.

NOAH: Help! One of the mice has fallen overboard!
JAPHETH: We'll have to give it mouse-to-mouse resuscitation.

What's the a definition of a caterpillar?
A worm rich enough to buy a fur coat.

NOAH: Come quick! One of the fleas has gone mad!
JAPHETH: You mean it's a loony-tick?

What's worse than a giraffe with a sore throat?
A centipede with sore feet.

What did the python say to his girlfriend?
"I've got a crush on you."

Mrs Noah was trying to get to sleep one night but she was kept awake by the squeaking of the mice. "What are you going to do about all that squeaking?" she asked Noah.

"Well," he said, "I'm not going to get up and oil them!"

Why did the fly fly?
Because the spider spied her.

SHEM: Help! One of the mice has just made a huge hole in the side of the Ark!
NOAH: What kind of mouse could make such a huge hole?
SHEM: A hippopotamouse.

A flea and a fly in a flue
Were imprisoned, so what could they do?
Said the fly, "Let us flee!"
Said the flea, "Let us fly!"
So they flew through a flaw in the flue.

What kind of food do snakes like best?
Hiss fingers.

What sweets do frogs like best?
Lollihops.

TALL STORIES

Gordon and Geraldine are the Ark's two resident giraffes. It's impossible to keep a secret from them because they're very nosey. That's because with their long necks they can look in windows and peer over walls to see what giraffeter! Here's a brief selection of their favourite giraffe jokes.

What's the highest form of animal life?
A giraffe.

GERALDINE: Why does Gordon have such a long neck?
NOAH: I don't know.
GERALDINE: Because his feet smell terrible.

What's tall and yellow and comes out in the spring?
A giraff-odil.

What kind of jokes do giraffes like best?
Tall stories.

JAPHETH: I've just crossed a giraffe and a hedgehog.
GORDON: And what have you got?
JAPHETH: The biggest toothbrush the world has ever seen.

What's worse than a giraffe with a sore throat?
A giraffe with a stiff neck.

Is a baby giraffe ever taller than its mother?
Only when it sits on its father's shoulders.

What do you call a giraffe who steps on your foot?
Anything you want – his head's so far away he can't hear you.

GERALDINE: Why do giraffes have such long necks?
NOAH: I don't know.
GERALDINE: To connect their heads to their bodies, silly!

Why do giraffes have such a tiny appetite?
Because a little goes a long, long way.

NOAH: If a giraffe gets wet feet, does it catch a cold?
MRS NOAH: Yes, I should think so, but not until a week later.

What do you get if you cross a giraffe with a dog?
A creature that barks at low-flying aircraft.

WOOF!!

ANIMAL CRACKERS

What always succeeds?
A toothless budgie.

MRS NOAH: These baby pigs are so greedy!
NOAH: That's because they want to make hogs of themselves.

What did the mother bee tell her naughty son?
"Bee-hive yourself!"

SHEM: What kind of fish does the pelican prefer?
JAPHETH: He's not fussy — anything will fit the bill.

What's a nightingale?
A windy evening.

MRS NOAH: Why are those owls looking so sad?
JAPHETH: Because it's too wet-to-woo.

What's the best way of catching a squirrel?
Act like a nut.

NOAH: That little oyster won't lend me five pounds.
JAPHETH: Why not?
NOAH: He's just shellfish.

Where do baby fish go every morning?
To plaice school.

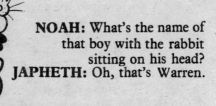

NOAH: What's the name of that boy with the rabbit sitting on his head?
JAPHETH: Oh, that's Warren.

SHEM: I wonder what the porcupines ate when I forgot to feed them?
JAPHETH: Whatever they could find.
SHEM: But what if they couldn't find anything?
JAPHETH: Then they'd eat something else.

What did the skunk say when the wind changed direction?
Oh dear, it's all coming back to me now.

Which animal bothers you in bed?
A night-mare.

MRS NOAH: What are those cows watching on TV?
NOAH: The evening moos.

Why is a rabbit's nose so shiny?
Because its powder puff is at the wrong end.

HAM: I swallowed a duckling just now!
NOAH: Oh, no! How do you feel?
HAM: A bit down in the mouth.

Where do American cows come from?
Moo York.

JAPHETH: I had a narrow squeak yesterday.
MRS NOAH: What happened?
JAPHETH: I almost trod on a mouse.

What happens to mad squirrels?
They get sent to the nut house.

MRS NOAH: I hope you washed that fish before you cooked it.
SHEM: Why should I? It's been swimming around in water all its life.

What do you call a cat who sucks lemons?
A sourpuss.

JAPHETH: I've just crossed a mouse and a bar of soap.
NOAH: And what did you get?
JAPHETH: Bubble and squeak.

What did one flea say to the other flea when they were going out?
Shall we walk or take a dog?

Where do flies go in winter?
To the glass factory where they're made into bluebottles.

SHEM: Why do those skunks keep arguing?
NOAH: Perhaps it's because they like raising a stink.

What did one pig say to the other?
"Let's be pen pals."

SHEM: These cows get on so well together.
JAPHETH: Yes, they're always giving each other a helping hand.
SHEM: I suppose it's what you'd call cow-operation.

Who is the chickens' favourite author?
Charles Chickens, author of Great Eggspectations.

NOAH: What's the best way to avoid insect bites?
JAPHETH: Basically, stop biting insects.

MRS NOAH: Why don't elephants ride bicycles?
SHEM: I don't know.
MRS NOAH: Because their thumbs are too big to work the bell.

What's the hardest key to turn?
A donkey.

JAPHETH: What's worse than a tortoise with claustrophobia?
MRS NOAH: I can't think.
JAPHETH: An elephant with hay fever.

JAPHETH: What's the name of that pony?
NOAH: Radish.
JAPHETH: So that's your horse Radish . . .

MRS NOAH: What games do cows play at parties?
NOAH: Moo-sical chairs.

What are small and furry and squeak when you pour milk on them?
Mice Krispies.

Why did the pelican put his feet in his mouth?
Because he wanted to foot the bill.

HAM: What's the best definition of an ant?
JAPHETH: I don't know.
HAM: An insect that works hard but still has time to go to picnics.

Why couldn't the dog go to the psychiatrist?
Because he wasn't allowed on the couch.

NOAH: Those two snails are fighting again.
JAPHETH: Are you going to do anything about it?
NOAH: No, I'll just leave them to slug it out.

Which animals have their eyes closest together?
The ones with the smallest heads.

NOAH: One of those crabs just bit my toe!
MRS NOAH: Which one?
NOAH: I can't tell, they all look the same to me.

What weighs a ton and jumps around like a frog?
A hoppy-potamus.

How many skunks do you need to make a stink?
Quite a phew!

NOAH: That chicken's a very tough character.
SHEM: That's because he came from a hard-boiled egg.

What do you call a horse with laryngitis?
A hoarse horse.

MRS NOAH: This horse needs a new tail.
NOAH: Where are we going to get one from?
MRS NOAH: The re-tail shop.

Why shouldn't you tell your secrets to a peacock?
Because they spread tails.

NOAH: What has twenty-two legs and two wings but cannot fly?
JAPHETH: A monster insect?
NOAH: No, a football team.

What do you call a rabbit that inspects rabbit holes?
A borough (burrow) surveyor.

SHEM: I've put my shirt on a horse.
JAPHETH: You idiot! You'll lose it.
SHEM: No I won't — it's a clothes horse!

What cat lives on the bottom of the ocean?
An octopuss.

NOAH: Have you heard the story of the three deer?
HAM: No.
NOAH: Oh dear, dear, dear . . .

Why was 1988 a good year for frogs and kangaroos?
Because it was a leap year.

NOAH: This dog loves melons!
HAM: I suppose you could call it a meloncollie . . .

Where do cattle go to eat?
The cow-feteria.

SHEM: Cat you name four animals of the cat family?
NOAH: Mummy, Daddy and two kittens.

Why is a tiger like the letter V?
Because he comes after U.

NOAH: We're running out of room to build new pig pens.
JAPHETH: Perhaps we could build them on top of each other?
NOAH: Yes, and make a styscraper!

SHEM: What's the difference between a fish and a piano?
NOAH: I don't know.
SHEM: You can't tuna fish.

DADDY BEAR: Who's eaten my porridge?
BABY BEAR: And who's eaten my porridge?
MUMMY BEAR: Stop moaning, you two — I haven't made it yet.

Why did the Navy feed its hens with dynamite?
To get mine layers.

MRS NOAH: Why is that ant dancing on the lid of the jam jar?
NOAH: Because it says "Twist to open."

What's green and slimy and goes "Hith"?
A snake with a lisp.

NOAH: That's rabbit stew.
SHEM: How could you tell without tasting it?
NOAH: I can see the hares in it.

JAPHETH: Of all the animals on the Ark, the polar bear is the cheapest to feed.
MRS NOAH: Why is that?
JAPHETH: Because he lives on ice.

Why was the pony unhappy?
Because every time it wanted something its mother said, "Neigh".

What happens when a dog gets a sore throat?
He's totally yelpless.

JAPHETH: I've taught this dog to beg.
HAM: Does he find it difficult?
JAPHETH: No, yesterday he came back with nearly twenty pounds.

SHEM: I'm not feeling very well.
JAPHETH: What's wrong with you?
SHEM: I work like a mule, eat like a pig, and sleep like a dog.
JAPHETH: Ts sounds as if you need to see a vet.

Why did the Ark go "Ouch"?
Because a crab pinched its bottom.

JAPHETH: I call this pig Ink.
NOAH: Why do you call him that?
JAPHETH: Because he's always running out of the pen.

Why does Mrs Noah let the horse sit on the cooker?
Because he feels at home on the range.

What did the boy octopus say to the girl octopus?
I want to hold your hand, your hand, your hand, your hand . . .

What do cows wear to go into battle?
Camooflage.

What's the principal part of a lion?
His mane.

NOAH: This roast beef is delicious. And have you noticed how friendly the dog is today? He keeps wagging his tail at me!
JAPHETH: That's because you're eating off his plate.

Where do the hogs keep their money?
In the piggy bank.

NOAH: What's that strange song the fish sing each sundown?
JAPHETH: I think it's "Salmon Chanted Evening".

JAPHETH: Help! Help! I just swallowed a sheep.
MRS NOAH: How are you feeling?
JAPHETH: Baa-aad.

What do you call a dozen angry dolphins?
Cross porpoises.

MRS NOAH: The hens have decided to put on a show. Are you coming to watch?
JAPHETH: Will it be any good?
MRS NOAH: They promise an egg-stravaganza.

JAPHETH: I've just crossed an Alsatian and an alligator.
MRS NOAH: And what did you get?
JAPHETH: I'm not sure, but the postman's not delivering any more mail.

How did the alligators win the football pools?
They got eight score jaws.

NOAH: These Spanish chickens are no good — I never get any eggs.
MRS NOAH: You need to give them the special command.
NOAH: What's that?
MRS NOAH: Olé!

How can you say "hungry horse" in just four letters?
MTGG

MRS NOAH: Who is that singing in such a low voice?
NOAH: It must be one of the fish.
MRS NOAH: But which one?
NOAH: The bass.

If a quadruped has four legs and a biped has two legs, what is a zebra?
Stri-ped.

SHEM: I just crossed a skunk and a boomerang.
NOAH: And what did you get?
SHEM: A disgusting smell that I can't get rid of.

NOAH: Come quick! Someone's run off with the baby octopus!
MRS NOAH: Oh, no! — Squidnappers!

Japheth was mucking out the elephants one day when Edna asked him if she could have a pencil and paper to write to her sister. "But elephants can't write," said Japheth.

"It doesn't matter," said Edna. "My sister can't read."

HAM: Does that teddy bear want another slice of cake?
SHEM: No, he's already stuffed.

JAPHETH: That newt keeps telling lies.
MRS NOAH: Why?
JAPHETH: He's an amphibian.

SHEM: I've just been fly fishing.
MRS NOAH: And did you catch anything?
SHEM: Yes, a four-pound bluebottle.

What time is it when a hippopotamus sits on your fence?
Time to get a new fence.

NOAH: Help! The lion has swallowed a roll of film!
MRS NOAH: Don't panic! Nothing serious will develop.

SHEM: I've crossed a hungry lion with a dog.
NOAH: And what did you get?
SHEM: A creature that eats people, then buries the bones.

SHEM: I entered this dog for a dog show and I won first prize.
JAPHETH: That's great!
SHEM: I suppose so — but I would have preferred it if the dog had won.

What do you call the pigs' laundry?
Hogwash.

JAPHETH: How can you say "rabbit" without using the letter R?
HAM: I give up.
JAPHETH: Bunny!

NOAH: Do we have any wild ducks on the Ark?
JAPHETH: No, but we have some tame ones and I can make them angry.

NOAH: I'd really like some crocodile shoes.
JAPHETH: They'll never fit — the crocodiles' feet are much bigger than yours!

NOAH: I hear the hyena eats nothing but little bits of metal.
JAPHETH: Yes — they're his staple diet.

How do the undersea police patrol the ocean bed?
In squid cars.

NOAH: I've just crossed a nasty little bug with the Union Jack.
MRS NOAH: And what did you get?
NOAH: A patrio-tick.

NOAH: Did I ever tell you about my forebears?
SHEM: No, but I've heard about the three bears . . .

Which two animals always go wherever Noah goes?
His calves.

Where do sheep do their Christmas shopping?
Wool-worth's.

SHEM: What did the blind hedgehog say to the deer?
NOAH: I've no idea.

When is Noah like a bird of prey?
When he watches his sons like a hawk.

SHEM: That bloodhound is a complete failure.
NOAH: Why?
SHEM: I cut my finger yesterday and it kept fainting.

What's black and white and goes around on eight wheels?
A penguin on roller skates.

SHEM: Quick! Someone's stepped on one of the insects!
MRS NOAH: Call for the antbulance.

NOAH: This lion has a stomach ache.
MRS NOAH: It must be someone he ate.

If we get honey from a bee, what do we get from wasps?
Waspberry jam.

What do angry mice send each other at Christmas?
Cross-mouse cards.

JAPHETH: There's something wrong with this frog.
SHEM: Oh, yes — it keeps coughing.
JAPHETH: Maybe it has a person stuck in its throat!

Which animal has antlers and wears white gloves?
Mickey Moose.

MRS NOAH: I never knew that poodle was French.
HAM: How could you tell?
MRS NOAH: It just said "Boux woux"!

Why is a tarantula in your bed like a fire?
Because the quicker they're put out, the better.

JAPHETH: I wonder why chickens have such short legs?
MRS NOAH: If they were any longer their eggs would be smashed by the drop to the ground.

MRS NOAH: Winter's on its way.
NOAH: How do you know?
MRS NOAH: I just milked the cow and got ice-cream.

What happened when the two oxen bumped into each other?
There was an occident.

NOAH: Which family does the walrus belong to?
HAM: I've no idea — no family I know has ever had one.

Which animal talks the most?
A yak.

MRS NOAH: I've just crossed a bee and some minced meat.
SHEM: And what did you get?
MRS NOAH: A humburger.

JAPHETH: What steps would you take if a bear was following you?
SHEM: Big ones!

Which insect kneels down before it eats?
The praying mantis.

NOAH: That chicken just threw an egg at me!
JAPHETH: She's a terrible practical yolker.

HYENA: I just swallowed a Yorkshire terrier!
OSTRICH: Are you choking?
HYENA: No, I'm serious.

What happened when Shem fell into a load of cement?
He became a hard man.

NOAH: Why are all those big black birds drunk?
SHEM: They've been in the crow-bar.

What did the short-sighted porcupine say when he bumped into a cactus?
I'm awfully sorry . . .

What's grey and can see just as well from either end?
A seal with its eyes shut.

What's the definition of streaky bacon?
A pig running round with no clothes on.

JAPHETH: Why are you crying?
HAM: The cow just tripped over.
JAPHETH: There's no point crying over spilt milk!

SHEM: Is it easy to milk a cow?
NOAH: Yes, any jerk can do it.

Japheth was showing off his lion-taming tricks. For one of them he put his head right in the lion's mouth. "Don't you get nervous when you do that?" asked Mrs Noah.

"Yes, I do," admitted Japheth. "I'm afraid of the dark."

Which animal never really dies?
A pig – because once he's dead you can cure him and save his bacon.

HAM: Have I ever told you about the time I came face to face with a tiger?

NOAH: No!

HAM: There I was, with the tiger just a few inches away from me and preparing to spring . . .

NOAH: What did you do?

HAM: I moved along to see what was in the next cage.

Have you heard about the tiger who had pedestrian eyes?
They looked both ways before crossing.

NOAH: What's wrong with that kangaroo — it looks exhausted.

MRS NOAH: Yes, it's out of bounds.

Why are sheep just like pubs?
Because they're full of baas.

Where do swallows live?
In a stomach.

MRS NOAH: I've made a pot of tea for the big cats.
JAPHETH: Is it their favourite blend?
MRS NOAH: Yes, it's Lyons Quick Brew.

Mrs Noah was out on deck one day when she was hit on the head by a little white ball. "Who threw that?" she asked angrily.

One of the horses came trotting over. "Sorry," he said, "we were just playing stable tennis."

What has one horn and gives lots of milk?
The milk lorry.

NOAH: Japheth just swallowed a frog!
MRS NOAH: My goodness! Has it made him sick?
NOAH: Sick? It almost made him croak!

NOAH: Why do all the geese follow the one leader when they fly off for the winter?
MRS NOAH: Maybe he's the one with the map.

SHEM: That's a very nice fur coat you're wearing, Mum.

MRS NOAH: Thank you.

SHEM: What kind of fur is it?

MRS NOAH: I'm not sure, but every time I walk past a dog the hem begins to wag.

Where do the frogs hang their hats and coats?
In the croakroom.

What note do you get if a piano-playing elephant falls down a coal mine?
A Flat Minor.

Why did the tortoise beat the hare in the race?
Because nothing goes faster than Shell.

SHEM: I just tickled the donkey.

JAPHETH: And did he enjoy it?

SHEM: No — but I got a big kick out of it.

What did the doe say to her children?
Hurry up, deers.

JAPHETH: The goldfish have decided to go into business.
NOAH: How are they going to start?
JAPHETH: On a small scale.

What did the lion say when he saw two hunters in a Land Rover?
Ah! Meals on wheels!

MRS NOAH: The kangaroo has appendicitis.
JAPHETH: What are we going to do?
MRS NOAH: Give it a hoperation.

Why did the hen go into the jungle?
Because it was an eggsplorer.

What's black and white and noisy?
A penguin playing the drums.

NOAH: Have you ever seen a cat make a rabbit hutch?
HAM: No, but I've seen a fox make a chicken run.

MRS NOAH: Why are all those cows lying in the sun?
JAPHETH: Because they like tanning their hides.

What happened to the horse that ate a lot of sugar cubes?
He got a lump in his throat.

FOUR-LEGGED FRIENDS

On the middle deck of the Ark live all the creatures with four legs. It's a noisey place, with the lions roaring and the pigs squealing and the cows mooing, but it's a lot of fun — as you can find out for yourselves!

Why do lions have fur coats?
*Because they'd
look silly in
plastic macs.*

NOAH: I'm going to try an experiment and cross this cup of cocoa with an elk.
MRS NOAH: What will that make?
NOAH: A chocolate moose — I hope!

What does Shem give the hedgehogs for breakfast?
Prickled onions.

SHEM: This milk tastes funny.
MRS NOAH: It's because the cow has lost her memory.
SHEM: Oh, so it's milk of amnesia, is it?

What did the pony say when he got to the end of his nose-bag?
"That's the last straw."

What would happen if pigs could fly?
The price of bacon would go up.

SHEM: Why does that pig keep walking up and down the deck while he reads poetry?
JAPHETH: He's rehearsing to go on the stage.
SHEM: What part is he playing?
JAPHETH: Hamlet!

How do the otters get around the Ark?
By otter-mobile.

SHEM: Did you see that fox trot?
MRS NOAH: No, but I saw the goose step!

What animal has two humps and is found at the North Pole?
A very lost camel.

NOAH: What's the name of the pig over there?
JAPHETH: Fountain.
NOAH: Is that his real name?
JAPHETH: No, it's his pen name.

MRS NOAH: Those two rabbits want to get married.
NOAH: And after that I suppose they want to go on bunnymoon!

What do you call a male cow who's in charge of the police force?
The Chief Constabull.

HAM: Did you hear that one of the lions swallowed a table lamp last night?
NOAH: My goodness — what happened?
HAM: It's all right — he spat it out and now he's de-lighted.

What's the biggest milk-giver in Russia?
Moscow.

JAPHETH: Did you water the horses?
NOAH: Yes.
JAPHETH: Then I'll go and milk the cats.

What kind of donkeys have the shortest legs?
The smallest ones.

JAPHETH: I think I'll keep the skunks under my bed.
MRS NOAH: But what about the smell?
JAPHETH: They'll soon get used to it.

What's white, hairy and smells of peppermint?
A polo bear.

NOAH: What's the difference between a buffalo and a bison?
JAPHETH: You can't wash your hands in a buffalo.

What happened when Shem poured boiling water over the rabbit hutch?
He had Hot Cross Bunnies.

On the first day that the animals arrived on the Ark, they took some time to get to know one another. The tiger, who was a bit of a bully, walked round introducing himself. First he met a kangaroo. "Kanga," he said, showing his claws, "tell me who is the King of the Jungle."

"You are, Mr Tiger," said the kangaroo. "No doubt about that." The tiger walked on, and the next animal he met was a chimpanzee.

"Chimp," he said, lashing his tail, "tell me who is the King of the Jungle."

"You are, Mr Tiger," said the chimp. "No problem." On strolled the tiger, through the Ark, until he came to the place where the elephants had made their home.

"Elephant!" roared the tiger, showing his magnificent white teeth, "can you tell me who is the King of the Jungle?" The elephant didn't say anything. Instead he just bent down and wrapped his long trunk around the tiger, then picked him up and shook him hard. Then he banged his head against the side of the Ark and finally he threw him down the stairs. The tiger landed with a terrible thump and just lay there groaning for a while.

"Okay, okay," he said at last, picking himself up off the floor. "Just because you don't know the answer, there's no need to get violent!"

What did the beaver say when he chewed a hole in the side of the Ark?
"It's been nice gnawing you."

NOAH: One of the horses isn't feeling well.
MRS NOAH: Is it seriously ill?
NOAH: Yes, it needs to go to horsepital.

What did the donkey say when he had to eat thistles?
"I suppose thistle have to do."

HAM: That horse is such a sensible animal!
JAPHETH: Oh yes, he's pretty stable.

NOAH: Which of the animals would you rather be eaten by — a tiger or a crocodile?
JAPHETH: I'd prefer it if the tiger ate the crocodile.

What's the difference between a bear that's asleep and a bear that's awake?
With some of them it's impossible to tell the difference.

113

Ham and Shem were up on deck eating their lunchtime sandwiches when one of the baby monkeys came swinging down from the sails and tried to steal the food. "Shall I throw him a bit?" asked Shem.

"If you want," said Ham. So Shem picked up the monkey and threw it over the side.

Where do you find lesser-spotted leopards?
It depends where you left them.

SHEM: That camel looks depressed.
MRS NOAH: Don't worry — he's just got the hump.

The two skunks had been very naughty and escaped from their cage, and Japheth had been searching for them all morning. Finally he tracked them down in the bows of the Ark. "Oh dear," said one skunk nervously to the other, "here he comes and he looks furious! He's going to be so angry — what are we going to do?"

The second skunk thought for a moment, then said, "Let us spray . . ."

NOAH: Shem, stop pulling that lion's tail!
SHEM: I'm not pulling — he is!

What star sign are all cows born under?
Taurus.

What did the bull say to the cow?
When I fall in love it will be for heifer.

Japheth came racing down to the cabin one afternoon. "I can't believe it!" he said, looking worried. "One of the wolves has just been killed by a guinea pig."

"A guinea pig killed a wolf?" said Mrs Noah disbelievingly. "How could a guinea pig kill a wolf?"

"It got stuck in the wolf's throat and choked him."

How does Noah count all the cows on board the Ark?
He uses a cowculator.

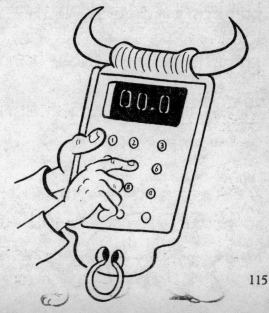

HAM: The polar bears' lunch is ready!
JAPHETH: What are they having?
HAM: Their favourite — ice-burgers.

What did the reindeer say before he told a joke?
This one's going to sleigh you.

JAPHETH: One of the green parrots is dead.
MRS NOAH: What happened to it?
JAPHETH: I washed it in biological soap flakes.
MRS NOAH: And the soap flakes killed it?
JAPHETH: No, it was the spin drier that finished it off.

What happened to the hyena who ate a jar of Bovril?
He made a laughing stock of himself.

JAPHETH: Why shouldn't you hold a tiger by the tail?
NOAH: I don't know.
JAPHETH: Because it may only be his tail — but it could be the end of *you!*

What did Mrs Noah give the pony when he didn't feel well?
Cough stirrup.

Can you milk a hamster?
Yes, but getting a bucket under it is tricky.

MRS NOAH: What's the name of that baby bear?
NOAH: I don't know — he's too shy to tell me.

NOAH: One of those bears is standing on its head!
JAPHETH: Yes — that's Yoga Bear.

How did Noah find the lost rabbit?
He made a noise like a carrot.

What's huge, grey and sits on the top deck of the Ark, mumbling?
The mumbo-jumbo.

One of the animals on board the Ark was a mouse called June. She was always playing tricks on the other animals, and then one day she was stupid enough to nibble the tail of one of the tigers. The next day was the first of July. Can you say why?
Because that was the end of June.

What's the safest sort of lion?
A dandelion.

What did Noah call the three-humped camel?
Humphrey.

MRS NOAH: I wonder how the sheep keep so warm in winter.
NOAH: Easy — they've got central bleating.

HAM: If an African tiger and an African lion had a fight, which do you think would win?
JAPHETH: Neither — because there are no tigers in Africa.

What are the worst-dressed animals on the Ark?
The horses – they wear shoes but no socks.

NOAH: Do you want to hear the story of the three little pigs?
SHEM: What is it?
NOAH: A pigtail.

NOAH: Why does that rabbit keep parachuting from the mast?
JAPHETH: He's a member of the Hare Force.

NOAH: Why are you eating grass?
JAPHETH: It's good for the eyesight.
NOAH: How do you know that?
JAPHETH: When did you last see a cow wearing glasses?

What's the best way of keeping baby dogs quiet?
Give them Hush-Puppies.

What did one sheep say to the other sheep as they walked up the gangplank?
After ewe.

HAM: Why do the lions eat raw meat?
SHEM: Have you tried teaching them to cook?

What kind of animals make the worse dancers?
Those with four legs – because they have two left feet.

Mrs Noah was sitting knitting one day when there was a quiet knock at the door and a tortoise came in. "Hello," said Mrs Noah. "Can I help you?"

The tortoise went pink. Finally it managed to say, "I'm terribly shy and I haven't made any friends on the Ark. I'm getting so lonely. Can you do anything about it?"

"Oh yes, my dear," said Mrs Noah. "We'll soon get you out of your shell."

NOAH: We've only got one elephant. Where are we going to get another?
MRS NOAH: How about a jumbo sale?

What's black, white and red all over?
An embarrassed zebra.

NOAH: What are the two bears called?
HAM: One's called Rupert the Bear and the other is called Winnie the Pooh.
NOAH: And do they have anything in common?
HAM: Only their middle names.

What's the difference between a sick cow and a dead bee?
One is a seedy beast and the other is a bee deceased.

NOAH: Why are the cows going "woof-woof"?
HAM: They're learning a foreign language.

What animal is Noah like when he takes a shower?
A little bear.

The polar bear family were out on the top deck of the Ark. "Mummy, Mummy," said the baby bear, "are you sure I'm really a true polar bear?"

"Yes, of course you are, darling," said his mother. "I'm a polar bear and Daddy's a polar bear, so you must be a polar bear too. Why do you ask?"

"Because I'm freezing cold!"

NOAH: Don't play cards with that big cat.
HAM: Why not?
NOAH: Because it's a cheetah.

What do the animals read on the Ark?
Gnus papers.

MRS NOAH: That sheep behaves just like a person.
SHEM: That's because she wants to be a eweman being.

SHAGGY DOG STORIES

Now for some longer jokes. Why long jokes are sometimes called shaggy dog stories, no one seems to know. But as you'll see, not all the jokes are about dogs and not all the dogs mentioned in them are shaggy. In fact, there are only two things these jokes have in common. They're all about animals — and they're all funny!

Once upon a time there was a teddy bear who made his living by working as a builder. One afternoon he came back from his lunch break to discover that someone had stolen his equipment. The teddy bear went straight to see the site foreman. "How am I supposed to get any work done?" he complained. "Someone has stolen my pick!"

"Don't worry," said the foreman. "Perhaps you didn't know, but today's the day the teddy bears have their picks nicked."

A man walked into a pet shop and asked the man behind the counter for one hundred beetles, fifty spiders and ten mice. "I've got the mice," said the pet shop owner, "but I'm afraid we don't stock beetles and spiders. Why do you need them?"

"Well," said the man, "I'm moving out of my flat today and the landlord told me I was to leave it exactly as I found it."

There was once a magician who used a parrot in his act. This parrot had seen the magic show hundreds of times and it used to get terribly bored having to sit on its perch, waiting for its trick to come round. One summer, for a change, the magician got a job on a cruise liner. Every evening he gave a magic show for the passengers, pulling rabbits out of hats, making volunteers from the audience disappear and making glasses and handkerchiefs vanish. "Here I have a gold watch," said the magician. "I'll wrap it in this magic scarf — and hey presto! It's gone!" The parrot, who'd seen the trick a hundred times before, squawked,

"It's in your pocket! It's in your pocket!"

The audience laughed and the magician was furious. For his next trick he made a golf ball disappear. "Abracadabra — and it's vanished!" he cried.

"No it hasn't," shrieked the parrot. "It's up your sleeve!"

The parrot went on being naughty until one night, when the magician was in the middle of his act, there was a terrible explosion. The passengers ran screaming for the lifeboats and in just a few minutes the ship had sunk without trace. Luckily the magician managed to escape in time and he sat forlornly on a liferaft bobbing around in the sea. From above his head there was a flutter of wings and the parrot landed next to him. The parrot stared at the magician with a puzzled look on its face. Eventually, after a long silence, it said, "Okay, I'll admit that was a brilliant new trick. What did you do with the ship?"

A motorist was driving down a quiet country lane one day when there was a terrible noise from his engine and his car suddenly stopped. The man leapt out, lifted the bonnet and peered anxiously inside, but he couldn't see anything wrong. "It's probably your carburettor seized up," said a deep voice over his shoulder. "You'll have to call out a mechanic."

The man looked round and found a big black and white cow standing behind him. "Definitely the carburettor," said the cow. The man was amazed. He began to walk down the lane in the direction of the nearest house and as he got close an old man came out.

"I can't believe my eyes," said the motorist. "I've just met a cow and it told me why my car had broken down."

The old man shook his head. "Was it a big black and white cow?"

"Yes," said the motorist. "She said my carburettor had seized up."

The old chap shook his head. "That's Daisy. You don't want to take any notice of her — she doesn't know anything about car mechanics."

When the Noah family went to see the travelling circus they were very impressed to find a dog playing the trombone. When the show was over Noah went to the stage door to find out more about this remarkable animal. "How did your dog learn to play?" he asked the trainer.

"Oh, it's no mystery," said the trainer. "He's been taking lessons for years."

An Australian on holiday in London saw an advertisement for a restaurant that boasted it could supply any meal that anyone requested. Determined to try it out for himself, he booked a table and went along. "What would you like for dinner, sir?" asked the waiter.

"I'd like a kangaroo sandwich," said the man, trying to think of something the restaurant would not be able to serve.

"Certainly, sir," said the waiter and off he went to the kitchen. Five minutes later he was back. "I'm afraid that the kangaroo sandwich is off," he announced.

"Ah-ha!" said the Australian, "Your advert said you could serve any meal I asked for but I've caught you out."

"You certainly have, sir," said the waiter. "We've run out of bread."

A man on safari in the African bush was stupid enough to get out of his Land Rover and go wandering around on his own. Suddenly a huge lion jumped out from behind the undergrowth, licking its lips and looking very ferocious. The man fell to his knees and began to pray, "Please God, don't let the lion eat me."

And when he looked up he found the lion was on its knees too, saying its prayers. "It's a miracle!" said the man.

"Thank you, God, for saving me!"

At that moment a voice came from above. "Sorry, but the lion *is* going to eat you. He's just saying grace before he begins."

"Do you want to have a look at my picture?" asked Shem.

"What have you painted?" asked Mrs Noah.

"It's a picture of a donkey eating grass."

"But where's the grass?"

"The donkey ate it all."

"And where's the donkey?"

"It's gone, because there's no point in staying around when there's no more grass to eat!"

A lady dashed into an ironmonger's shop and went straight to the front of the queue. "I'd like a mouse trap, please," she said. The assistant went off to find one, and was gone for several minutes.

"Please hurry up," said the lady, "I've got to catch a bus."

"I'm sorry, madam," said the assistant, "but we haven't got any traps big enough for that."

Ham, Shem and Japheth were out for a walk one Sunday afternoon when they came across a gloomy old castle. They crossed the drawbridge, and as soon as they were inside there was a flash of lightning and a puff of blue smoke, and a wizard appeared. "This is your lucky day," he said. "I'm going to give you all the chance to have a wish come true. All you have to do is spend an hour in my dark, dank, horrible dungeon. If you manage to stay there for an hour, you will be granted your heart's desire."

Ham was the first one into the dungeon. It was freezing and pitch black, but worst of all there was the most horrible smell he'd ever encountered. So he held his nose and waited for an hour, saying to himself, "I wish to be an artist and paint wonderful pictures." Sure enough, an hour later he emerged an artist.

Shem was the next one in and he, too, was stunned by the terrible smell. But like his brother he held his nose and kept wishing his wish. "I want to be a doctor, I want to be a doctor," he said. And lo and behold, an hour later he walked out of the dungeon a doctor.

Japheth was last one to get his chance. He walked into the dungeon and he smelled the dreadful pong, and the first thing he said was, "Pooh!" And at that moment there was a flash of lightning and a puff of blue smoke and he turned into — a bear!

Two billy goats were grazing in a field when they came across some rubbish that had been dumped — and being goats, they munched their way through all of it. Among the rubbish were some reels of film, which they ate. "Mmm!" said one goat, picking bits of celluloid from between its teeth, "That was rather good, wasn't it?"

"To be honest," said the other, licking its lips, "I preferred the book."

A lady was walking past a pet shop one day when she saw a very unusual purple bird sitting in the window, so she slipped inside. "Can you tell me what type of bird that is?" she asked.

"It's a munchbird, madam," replied the pet shop owner. "I'll show you why he's called a munchbird." He held up a pen and called, "Munchbird, my pen!" The bird flew across the shop, took the pen and ate it.

"Munchbird, my watch!" And the munchbird flew over, picked up the watch and with a single gulp swallowed it down.

"What a wonderful bird," said the lady. "Think how useful he'd be for getting rid of rubbish. I'll buy him!"

So she bought the munchbird and took it home. Later that day her husband came home from work. "What sort of bird is this?" he asked when he saw it.

"It's a munchbird and it will eat anything," said his wife.

"Munchbird, my foot!" said the man.

One fine sunny day a squid was swimming through the ocean when he bumped into his friend the whale. "Hello there, Squid!" said the whale. "How are you feeling today?"

"Not very well," said the squid. "I've had a virus and I can't seem to shake it off."

"Poor you," said the whale. "When I'm feeling under the weather I find that it helps if I swim at the bottom of the ocean, in the deepest water. Why don't you try that?"

"I don't like swimming that deep on my own," said the squid.

"I'll come down with you," said the whale, and so the two of them dived deeper in the water, down and down to the dark bottom. "This way," said the whale, and he led the squid to the mouth of a dark cave. As they approached there was a silvery flash of light and a huge shark, the squid's arch-enemy, came gliding out of the cave.

"Hello there, Shark!" said the whale. "I've brought that sick squid I owe you."

A very angry man walked into a pet shop dragging a dog behind him. "Ever since I bought this dog he's been making terrible messes all over the house, but I only bought him because you said that he was house-trained."

"He is," said the pet shop owner. "He won't go anywhere else."

Two ramblers were on a country walk when they discovered that the path crossed a field in which there was a very large bull. They'd just climbed the stile when they saw the farmer coming down the path. "Is the bull safe?" asked one rambler.

"Well," said the farmer, "I'd say he was much safer than you are."

A Frenchman, a German and a Scotsman were walking through the countryside one day when they saw a cow in a field. "Oh, look!" said the Frenchman. "Zere is a nice French cow."

"Zat iz not a French cow," said the German. "Zat is a German cow."

"You're both wrong," said the Scotsman. "It's a Scottish cow and I can prove it."

"How?" asked the Frenchman and the German.

"Look underneath. It's carrying its bagpipes!"

A family went out for a meal in a restaurant. The servings were huge and at the end of the meal the little boy and girl had both left a lot of food. When the father called over the waiter to pay the bill he said, "I wonder if we could have a bag to take home our children's leftovers for the dog?"

"Wow! Does that mean we're going to have a dog?" asked the little boy.

For a birthday treat, Mr and Mrs Snail took their son to the pizza parlour for dinner. Their pizzas had just arrived when Mr Snail looked out of the window and saw that it had begun to rain and the sky was black, as if a terrible storm was on the way. "If we're not careful we'll all be soaked," he said to Sam. "Would you be a good boy and go home and fetch our umbrellas?"

"All right," said Sam. "Just promise me that you won't eat my pizza while I'm away."

"We promise," said his parents, so off he went. Darkness came, and the next morning the sun rose, and still he wasn't back. Another day passed, and then another. Finally Mr Snail turned to his wife. "I think we'd better eat Sam's pizza before it goes all mouldy," he said.

At that moment a voice from the door said loudly, "If you do that, I won't go and get the umbrellas."

There were once three hedgehogs called Foot, Foot-Foot and Foot-Foot-Foot. When they wanted to play in the park they had to cross a busy main road and one day, although they were terribly careful, Foot was run over by a car and squashed flat. You can imagine how upset Foot-Foot and Foot-Foot-Foot were, and for nearly two weeks they wouldn't go out to play in the park. Then one day Foot-Foot said to Foot-Foot-Foot, "There's no point in us staying indoors and moping all day. If Foot was alive he'd have wanted us to go out and enjoy ourselves. Life has to go on."

"I suppose you're right," said Foot-Foot-Foot to Foot-Foot. "But we're going to have to be more careful that ever before when we cross the road. After all, we've got one Foot in the grave already."

Two hunters were out in the Indian jungle when a massive tiger stepped out of the undergrowth in front of them. "Keep absolutely calm," said the first hunter. "Remember what we read in the book. If we stand still and stare hard at the tiger he'll turn and run away and then we can shoot him."

"That's all very well," said the second hunter. "You've read the book and I've read the book — but what if the tiger *hasn't* read the book?"

A talent scout was walking down Oxford Street one day when he heard music and saw an old man standing on the pavement with a dog and a donkey. The dog was playing the guitar and the donkey was singing, and while all this was was going on the old man was collecting money in his hat. The talent scout was so impressed by the act that he pulled out a contract and signed them on the spot. "Come to the television studio on Friday," he said. "I'm going to make you all stars and you'll earn millions of pounds."

On Friday the talent scout waited at the TV studio but the old man and the dog and the donkey didn't arrive. Eventually he went down Oxford Street to look for them and, sure enough, there they were — still playing for the people passing by.

"Why didn't you come to the studio?" asked the talent scout.

"I was feeling too guilty," said the old man. "You see, we fooled you but I didn't think I could bear to fool millions of television viewers."

"You mean this whole thing is just a trick?" asked the talent scout.

"Yes it is," said the old man. "You see, the donkey can't sing a single note. The dog's a ventriloquist."

Noah was out for a walk one day when he saw an old man coming towards him, pulling a box along the ground on a lead. "Poor old chap," thought Noah, "I'll just humour him."

As the old man came past, dragging his box, Noah bent down and patted it. "What a nice dog you've got," he said.

"It's not a dog," said the old chap, "it's a cardboard box."

"Oh," said Noah, feeling rather silly, "I'm sorry — I thought you were a bit simple, that's all." And he walked on.

When he'd gone the old man bent down and looked at the box. "Fooled him that time, Spot, didn't we?" he said.

One afternoon a girl took her pet dachshund to the cinema to watch *Gone With the Wind*. The usherette was about to throw the dog out when she noticed that it was enjoying the film, so she let it stay. It cried during the sad bits and pricked its ears at the exciting bits and had a wonderful time. At the end of the film she said to the girl, "I was amazed to see your dog enjoying the film so much."

"So was I," said the girl. "He hated the book."

A man was taken to the police station after he and his brothers had had a fight in their home. "It's not my fault," said the man. "Me and my three brothers all live in one room. One brother has five cats, one has five dogs and the other has a donkey — and they all live in the same room with us. The smell is dreadful. Can't you do something about it?"

"It sounds terrible," said the policeman. "Why don't you open the window?"

"What? And let all my pigeons fly away?" said the man.

A man was buying a horse from a farmer. "What commands do I give to this horse to make it stop and go?" he asked.

"Well," said the farmer, "it's rather unusual. To make the horse go you should say 'Few', and to make it stop you must say 'Amen'." The man thought it sounded strange but he bought the horse anyway and took it out for a ride.

"Few!" he cried, and the horse went trotting off — straight towards the edge of a cliff. "Help!" yelled the man, "I've forgotton the word for stop!" As the edge of the cliff got closer he closed his eyes and began to pray. "Please, Lord, save me from tumbling over the cliff. Amen." Instantly, just inches away from the edge, the horse stopped. The rider opened his eyes and saw a terrible drop beneath them.

He wiped his sweaty brow with the back of his hand. "Phew!" he said "That was a lucky esc—aaaaagh!"

Shem woke up one morning and went downstairs to the kitchen to make a cup of tea. He was just waiting for the kettle to boil when he heard a strange pecking sound at the back door. Outside on the doorstep was a cute little penguin, so Shem brought it in and gave it some sardines. When they'd both had breakfast he took the penguin to the police station. "What shall I do with this penguin?" he asked.

"Take it to the zoo," said the policeman.

"Okay," said Shem, so off he went to the zoo. Later that day he was walking down the High Street when he met the policeman again.

"I thought I told you to take that penguin to the zoo," said the policeman, pointing to the penguin who was waddling along at Shem's side.

"I did," said Shem, "and now I'm taking him to see *Rambo* at the pictures."

A man was out for a walk with his dog one day and decided to go for a meal in a restaurant. So in he went, taking the dog with him. He'd only just sat down when a waitress came up. "I'm sorry, but we don't allow dogs in this restaurant," she said.

"But please," said the man, "this is no ordinary dog. This dog can actually talk."

"I really don't care if he can sing 'Happy Birthday to You' while he's standing on his head!" said the waitress. "He's going to have to wait outside."

Just then the manager came up. "We're sorry, sir, but no dogs are allowed," he said.

"But I was just telling the waitress that it's not an ordinary dog," explained the man. "This dog can talk!"

The manager was getting very fed up. "All right," he said, "we'll see if you're telling the truth. Dog, what is there above this restaurant?"

"Rr-r-oof," said the dog.

"You see, sir," said the manager, getting annoyed, "it's just an ordinary dog and it can't talk. Now would the pair of you please leave?" The man and the dog got up and went back out into the street. As they stood on the pavement the dog looked up, then clapped its paw to its head in disgust.

"Now I understand what he meant," it said. "Look, above the restaurant there's a hairdressing salon!"

A furious farmer went to the market where the week before he had bought a cow. "The cow

you sold me last Wednesday is almost blind!"
he stormed. "You told me she was a good milker
and had a nice nature but you didn't tell me she
couldn't see."

"Oh yes I did," said the trader. "I told you
she didn't look too good."

Japheth went out one day and met a man who
was sprinkling grey powder all over the road.
"What are you doing?" asked Japheth.

"I'm scattering elephant powder," said the
man.

"But you don't need to," said Japheth.
"There aren't any elephants around here."

"That just proves how effective it is, doesn't
it?"

A visitor who was touring round a remote part
of Scotland found that he was marooned in a
village by very heavy rain which flooded the
road and caused a mud slide. He decided to go
to the pub for a drink and as he sat on his stool
he remarked to the barmaid. "This is like the
Flood."

"The what?" she asked

"The Flood. You know, the story of the
terrible rain and Noahs's Ark and all the
animals."

"Sorry," said the waitress, "I haven't read a
newspaper for weeks."

Two dodos stood on the seashore of Mauritius
and watched a huge cruiseliner dropping its
anchor in the bay. After a little while the
passengers were transferred to small launches

which came buzzing back to the shore.

"Watch out!" said one dodo, "We'd better hide."

"Why?" said the other.

"Because we're supposed to be extinct, stupid."

An American couple had taken the trip of a lifetime to Kenya, and they were on a safari to see all the wild animals. One day they were walking through the long grass and looking for some wildlife, when the biggest lion you've ever seen jumped out of a tree and grabbed the lady American in its huge teeth.

"Help!" she screamed. "Shoot! Shoot!"

"I can't!" yelled her husband in despair. "There's no film in the camera!"

Mrs Noah went to have a cup of coffee with her best friend Betty. They were sitting in the front room discussing *Neighbours* when Betty's little dog came in with her tail wagging. "Have you seen the *Sunday Telegraph*?" asked the dog.

"It's under the coffee table," said Betty and the dog went over, picked up the paper and walked out.

"That's incredible!" said Mrs Noah. "Is it true that your dog reads the paper?"

"No," said Betty. "She doesn't read it. She just likes looking at the pictures."

Have you heard the story about the time Shem went to an animal auction? A huge multi-coloured parrot caught his eye and he decided to bid for it — but there was someone else in the auction room who wanted the parrot too, and each time Shem made a bid they called out a higher one. The price went higher and higher, but Shem was determined to get the parrot so he kept going and eventually he got it, though he had to pay more than one hundred pounds. As he went to pay the auctioneer he asked, "Can the parrot talk?"

"Of course it can," said the auctioneer. "Who do you think has been bidding against you?"

An orchestra went on tour to Africa and one night, when all the other musicians went to bed, the violinist decided to go for a walk in the jungle in the dark. "You should take a gun," said one of his friends. "There are wild animals out there."

"I don't need a gun," said the violinist. "I shall take my violin and if I meet any animals I'll soothe them with a beautiful melody." So off he went. He hadn't gone far when he came to a jungle clearing where a huge elephant was standing, pawing at the ground and ready to charge. The violinist picked up his instrument and began to play so softly and sweetly that immediately the elephant stood enraptured, listening to the tune. Gradually dozens of other animals came creeping out of the jungle to listen too, and soon the violinist found himself surrounded by an audience of lions and cheetahs and crocodiles and rhinos and snakes and hippos and every kind of creature you can imagine.

They were all standing there listening to the beautiful music when suddenly a scruffy old lion came bounding up to the violinist and ate him in a single gulp. Everyone else was furious. "Why did you do that?" they demanded. "We were enjoying it!"

"Eh?" said the old lion. "Speak up, will you?"

A boy was out riding on his pony one day. They passed a field with a sheep in it, and as they went by the sheep said, "Good afternoon."

"Gosh!" said the boy, "I never knew that sheep could talk."

The pony turned his head so that he could see the boy and said, "You learn something new every day, don't you?"

A girl from the city went to stay on her grandfather's farm for the summer holidays. One day, Grandfather took her to see a field full of sheep. "All those sheep are mine," he said proudly. "Can you count how many there are?"

"One hundred and six," said the girl.

"That's amazing!" said Grandfather. "How did you manage to count them all so quickly?"

"It was easy," said his granddaughter. "First I counted all the legs, then I divided by four."

It was Cup Final in the jungle and hundreds of animals had gathered around the football pitch to watch the best match of the season. To a fanfare of trumpets from the elephants, the two rival teams walked out on to the turf. Jungle United were wearing green and white striped jerseys, while Jungle Rovers were in their best red strip. The captains tossed a coin to decide which end they were going to play, then the referee blew his whistle and they were off!

It was a terrific game and the crowd roared with excitement as each side put eight goals into the back of the net. With one minute to go the score was still eight-all when Boris Beetle, the Rovers' tiny but brilliant centre-forward, was passed the ball and began to race back down the field with it. He wrong-footed the United goalkeeper, lined up for his shot, and was just about to score when Henry the Hippo came down the pitch, made a leap for Boris — and squashed him as flat as a pancake.

"He's dead," declared the referee. "Penalty kick to the Rovers."

"Oh no, Ref! I didn't mean to kill him," pleaded Henry. "I was just going to tackle him."

A country lad had taken his cow to market but he hadn't been able to sell her so they were both walking home along the lanes. He hadn't got very far when a car drove up and stopped. "I can give you a lift if you'd like," said the stranger inside, "but I don't have room for your cow."

"Thanks," said the lad. "I'd like a lift and you don't have to worry about the cow. She'll follow us at her own speed." So in he got and off went the car at about thirty miles an hour.

"Good lord!" said the driver after a minute or two. "Your cow is keeping up with me." So he put his foot on the accelerator and the car increased speed to forty miles an hour. The driver looked back in the mirror — and there was the cow, still trotting along behind. "All right," said the motorist, and he put his foot down even further. Soon the car was speeding along at fifty miles an hour — and the cow was still running along right behind them!

"I'm a bit worried about your cow," said the driver after a few miles at this speed. "Her tongue is sticking out of the right side of her mouth. Is she all right?"

"Oh yes," said the country lad. "When she sticks her tongue out like that it means she's going to overtake!"

A man went into a pet shop and saw a monkey swinging about from a wire in the middle of the ceiling. "What's that monkey doing there?"

asked the man.

"Just ignore him," said the pet shop owner. "He's totally crazy. He thinks he's a lightbulb."

"Well, why don't you bring him down from there and put him in a cage?" asked the customer.

"What?" said the pet shop owner. "And serve the customers in the dark?"

Ham and Shem went to the market and came back with two horses. "They look very much alike," said Shem, looking at them. "How are we going to be able to tell them apart?"

We'll tie a red ribbon round my horse's neck," said Ham.

"Good idea," said Shem. But the next day they came back to the field and found that the ribbon had fallen off.

"How shall we tell which one's which now?" asked Ham.

"I know," said Shem. "I'll have the brown one and you can have the black one."

A little mouse went into a shop that sold musical instruments and squeaked to the owner, "I'd like to buy a mouse-organ, please." As you can imagine, the shop owner was astonished at this.

"I've been running this shop for nearly twenty years," he said, "and I've never had a mouse come and ask for a mouse-organ until today. And here you are, the second mouse to ask for one in a single day! Only an hour or two ago a grey mouse came asking for a mouse organ . . . "

"Oh yes," said the little mouse. "That was our Monica (harmonica)."

It was a cold, wet, windy evening when the knight arrived at an isolated pub in the middle of Dartmoor. He staggered in the front door and the locals helped him into a chair by the fire while the landlord went to get him a hot drink and a meal. "Thank you," said the knight. "My name is Sir Galahad and I need your help. I'm on a mission to save a damsel from a dragon, but my horse has gone lame and if I'm not careful I'll be too late to save her. Can any of you lend me a mount?"

Everyone shook their heads sadly, because none of them had a horse. "A donkey?" asked the knight. "Surely there must be *something* in this village that I can ride?" The landlord thought for a minute.

"We've got a very shaggy old Irish wolfhound," he said after a while. "I suppose you could try riding that." And he went behind the bar and came back with a huge, very scruffy and dirty dog. The knight climbed on its back and found that it could carry him, and the landlord was just about to open the door and wave them off into the stormy dark when his wife came bustling into the bar.

"What are you doing?" she asked, and they told her. "But that dog is far too scruffy for Sir Galahad. I couldn't possibly let a knight out on a dog like this!" she said.

FINGS WITH WINGS

Here's a question for you to answer. Why is there no honey on the Ark? Because there are no b's in ark! This isn't strictly true, of course, because there are two of every creature you can think of on the Ark — and here's a collection of jokes about those that can fly.

What happened when Shem ran over the budgie with a lawnmower?
There was shredded tweet all over the place.

SHEM: Help! Help! We've lost one of the canaries!
MRS NOAH: We'd better send for the Flying Squad.

Where do birds live on the Ark?
In the crow's-nest.

Why don't ducks fly upside down?
Because it makes them quack up.

Do ducks make good decorators?
No, they just paper over the quacks.

What did Mrs Noah give the sick budgie?
Tweetment.

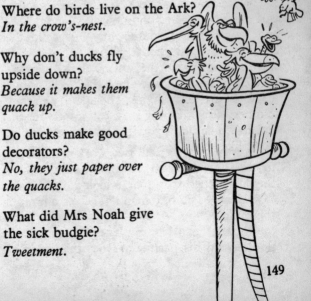

149

JAPHETH: Why did the chicken cross the road?
NOAH: I don't know.
JAPHETH: For some fowl reason.

SHEM: Do you know anyone who's been on the TV?
JAPHETH: My parrot, but he's house-trained now.

MRS NOAH: I'm very worried about this cat. It thinks it's a chicken.
NOAH: Maybe we should take it to the vet?
MRS NOAH: But it lays such wonderful eggs . . .

What has four legs and can fly?
Two birds.

Before the Ark set sail, two workmen came to install some nice carpets in the cabin. When they'd finished they took a look at their work. "Oh dear," said one man. "There's a lump in the middle."

"I must have left my bag of crisps on the floor," said his partner. "Does this mean we have to take the whole carpet up and start again?"

"No, I know how we can solve the problem." And the workman took a big hammer and bashed the lump until it was quite flat and the carpet was smooth again.

At that moment Mrs Noah came out of the galley with a cup of coffee for each of them. "I thought you might like this," she said. "And here are your crisps — you left them in the hall. By the way, I don't suppose either of you have seen the budgie anywhere, have you?"

What do geese watch on television?
Duckumentaries.

What kind of seagull can't fly?
A bi-seagull.

MRS NOAH: This budgie is almost blind.
JAPHETH: I'll get him some glasses.
MRS NOAH: Where can you get them from?
JAPHETH: The Birds-Eye shop.

What did the parrot say to the spaniel?
"I'm a cocker too (cockatoo)."

SHEM: This wasp is sick.
NOAH: We'll send it to a waspital.

Why is there an eagle on the lectern at the church?
Because it's a bird of prey.

MRS NOAH: Did you hear the story of the peacock?

HAM: No.

MRS NOAH: Oh, it's a beautiful tail . . .

Why wasn't the butterfly allowed into the dance?

Because it was a moth ball.

MRS NOAH: Will you get me a box of ducks for Christmas?

NOAH: Why do we need a box of ducks for Christmas?

MRS NOAH: We can't celebrate without Christmas quackers!

Which bird starts on two legs and ends up on four?

A chicken – which ends up on the dining table.

SHEM: This budgie lays square eggs.
MRS NOAH: That's amazing!
SHEM: And it talks too.
MRS NOAH: That's incredible! What does it say?
SHEM: "Oooh, ouch!"

What do bees say in summer?
"'S warm!"

SHEM: That duck's a fast mover!
JAPHETH: Yes, he's a real quick quack.

What did the duckling say when she emerged from the shell?
"What an egg-sperience!"

HAM: What's the difference between a duck and a goose?
NOAH: Ducks go "quack" and geese go "honk".
HAM: So, say you were out for a walk and you saw a flock of birds going "honk, honk" — what would you do?
NOAH: I'd pull in and let them pass.

Why do chickens watch television?
They like good hentertainment.

Why did Ham put the chicken in a hot bath?
In the hope that she'd lay boiled eggs.

NOAH: I once had a lovely parrot. It could copy any voice it heard.
MRS NOAH: And what happened to it?
NOAH: I was once stranded on a desert island and had to eat it.
MRS NOAH: And what did it taste like?
NOAH: Chicken, turkey, pheasant . . . that bird could imitate anything!

Which bird is good at getting into Turkish houses?
A turkey.

MRS NOAH: Why are those ducks crowded round the radio like that?
JAPHETH: They're listening to the feather forecast.

What's black, white and red and bounces up and down?
A sunburnt penguin on a pogo stick.

SHEM: Why is this chicken refusing to lay eggs?
MRS NOAH: She says she's not working for chicken feed.

Japheth was showing off his favourite parrot, which he'd been training to speak. "Look, Mum," he said. "If I pull its left leg it sings 'Happy Birthday to You'. And if I pull its right leg it sings 'We Wish You a Merry Christmas'."

"I'm very impressed," said Mrs Noah, "but what happens if you pull both legs at once?"

"I fall over, you silly idiot!" shrieked the parrot.

What birds live in coal pits?
Miner birds.

What should you call a bee
born in May?
A maybe.

What happened when the
parrot swallowed a clock?
It became a politic-ian.

Where do parrots with three
"A" levels go?
Polytechnic.

NOAH: What's green, hairy and noisy and
turns into the biggest butterfly you've ever
seen?
SHEM: I've no idea.
NOAH: A caterpillar tractor.

What do you get if you cross a parrot with a
woodpecker?
A bird that knocks on doors and delivers messages.

JAPHETH: I feel sorry for that pelican.
MRS NOAH: Why?
JAPHETH: Well, wherever he goes he always
has that big bill facing him.

MRS NOAH: I think I'll hold a party for the
chickens.
HAM: I shouldn't bother.
MRS NOAH: Why?
HAM: Because it's difficult to make hens meet.

HAM: Did you see that duckway we just passed?
NOAH: What's a duckway?
HAM: About three pounds.

Which bird can lift the heaviest weights?
The crane.

NOAH: What should we feed the parrots?
JAPHETH: Polyfilla.

JAPHETH: I made a terrible mistake! Last week I fed the hens on sawdust.
NOAH: And what happened?
JAPHETH: This morning their eggs hatched — and we've got nine chicks and a woodpecker.

Why did Noah refuse to put the sick eagle in the hold of the Ark?
Because it would have been an illegal cargo.

MRS NOAH: I've cooked some chicken that will tickle your palate.
NOAH: How have you cooked it?
MRS NOAH: I've left the feathers on.

MRS NOAH: That crow is completely mad!
NOAH: Yes, he's a raven lunatic.

Where do well-behaved turkeys go when they die?
To oven.

Why do birds in nests always agree?
Because they don't want to fall out.

HAM: That turkey is like a wicked little creature.
SHEM: Why do you say that?
HAM: Because it's always goblin'.

Which animal is the cheapest to keep?
A moth – because it eats nothing but holes.

MRS NOAH: I've just made the chicken soup.
NOAH: Thank goodness — I thought it was for *our* lunch.

What's the opposite of a cock-a-doodle do?
A cock-a-doodle don't.

JAPHETH: I'd like to buy a chicken for the Ark.
FARMER: Do you want a pullet?
JAPHETH: No, I'll carry it home carefully.

What's the favourite food of geese?
Gooseberries.

What sort of birds can you find in captivity?
Jail-birds.

What do you call a bee who buzzes strangely?
A mumble bee.

MRS NOAH: That chicken's very red in the face.
NOAH: Yes, it's henbarrassed.

Why did the turkey cross the road?
To prove it wasn't chicken.

Why do bees hum?
Because they don't know the words.

Why do bees buzz?
Because they can't whistle.

NOAH: Why is this bird always moping about?
JAPHETH: Because it's a bluebird.

Where do cockerels go if they lose their knees?
To London – because there are lots of Cockneys there.

Two hens were having a conversation as they sat roosting on the deck of the Ark. "I'm so proud of my son," said one. "He's passed his exams to become a *hen*gine driver."

"So what?" said the second. "My son's a trained *hen*gineer."

NOAH: If a turkey walked across the road, crossed back again, then went swimming in a muddy puddle, what would you have?
MRS NOAH: I've no idea.
NOAH: A dirty double-crosser.

MRS NOAH: I'm never walking past that hen-house again.
JAPHETH: Why?
MRS NOAH: I can't bear the foul language.

Why is bees' hair so sticky?
Because they use honey combs.

NOAH: I've just been stung by one of your bees!
JAPHETH: Show me which one did it and I'll tell it off.

Which bird is always out of breath?
A puffin.

Why do birds fly south in winter?
Because it's too far to walk.

On which side does a chicken have most feathers?
The outside.

SHEM: Those chickens are always laughing.
NOAH: It's because of that one there.
SHEM: Why?
NOAH: It's a real comedihen.

What goes zzub-zzub?
A bee flying backwards.

JAPHETH: That Scottish owl is really angry.
SHEM: Why is that?
JAPHETH: Because I won't let him hoot at night.

Where do wasps come from?
Stingapore.

IT'S RAINING CATS AND DOGS

The Noah family love their pets — which explains why there are so many cats and dogs living on the Ark!

What kind of cat will you find in a library?
A catalogue.

HAM: What's that dog's name?
JAPHETH: Camera.
HAM: Why's that?
JAPHETH: He's always snapping.

What should you give a Greek cat for dinner?
Mouse-aka.

HAM: Why is that cat so small?
JAPHETH: Mum keeps feeding it condensed milk.

When is a black dog not a black dog?
When it's a greyhound.

HINK!!

MRS NOAH: There's a cat burglar on this Ark.
NOAH: How do you know?
MRS NOAH: We've been robbed — and all that's missing is a bottle of milk and a saucer.

What happened to the cat that swallowed a ball of wool?
She had mittens.

SHEM: What are you doing?
NOAH: I'm playing chess with this dog.
SHEM: That's amazing! He must be a very clever dog.
NOAH: Not really — I've beaten him three times already.

Why did the poor dog chase his tail?
He was trying to make ends meet.

NOAH: Why is that dog called Johann Sebastian?
HAM: Haven't you heard him Bach?

What did the idiot call his Dalmatian dog?
Stripe.

HAM: Why is this dog in such a bad mood?
NOAH: Ignore him — he's just got distemper.

Mrs Noah was beginning to worry about her son Japheth. He was acting like a dog! He liked eating dog food, he gnawed bones, and whenever anyone came in the cabin door he barked and showed his teeth. "We'll have to take him to the doctor," said Mrs Noah, and eventually they managed to find one who could help. After a few weeks Japheth was getting back to normal. He couldn't stand the taste of dog food, he gave up bones and when people came into the room he didn't bark. The doctor eventually decided that he was well enough to give up the treatment.

"Thank you for helping him," said Mrs Noah. "He's so much better. Just feel how cold and wet his nose is."

Why are cats so difficult to please?
Because they are purrfectionists.

JAPHETH: I think there's something wrong with me — I feel as if I'm a cat.
NOAH: How long have you felt like this?
JAPHETH: Ever since I was a kitten.

PURRRR

Why don't cats shave?
Because tests show that nine out of ten cats prefer Whiskas.

JAPHETH: Would you like to play with this new dog?
NOAH: Does it bite?
JAPHETH: That's what I want to find out.

What did the cat say as it went down the fast lane of the M25?
Meeeeee-OW!

NOAH: Have you put the cat out?
MRS NOAH: Oh no, it wasn't on fire *again*, was it?

Where should you take a sick dog?
To the dogtor.

SHEM: Hey! This dog can do maths!
NOAH: I don't believe it.
SHEM: Well, I've just asked him what ten minus ten is, and he said nothing.

What do cats rest their heads on at night?
Caterpillars.

What do cats eat for breakfast?
Mice Krispies.

MRS NOAH: Help! We've lost one of the dogs.
NOAH: Let's put an advert in the *Ark Daily News*.
MRS NOAH: That's no good — the dog can't read.

If a husky can stand the lowest temperatures, which type of dog can stand the highest?
A hot dog.

JAPHETH: Have you got anything to cure my dog's fleas?
MRS NOAH: It depends on what's wrong with the fleas.

NOAH: My dog has no nose.
MRS NOAH: How does he smell?
NOAH: Terrible!

Why did the dog sit in the corner each time the doorbell rang?
Because he was a boxer.

JAPHETH: Does that dog have fleas?
NOAH: I'm not sure. He's so lazy that even if he did he wouldn't bother to scratch them.

What do you call a cat that comes from the Wild West?
A posse.

FIRST DOG: My name's Spot. What are you called?
SECOND DOG: I'm not sure but I think it might be Get Down Boy.

Ham was reading a book all about mountains one night when he asked, "Dad, have you ever seen the Catskill Mountains?"

"No I haven't," said Noah, "but I've seen the cats kill mice."

167

Did you hear about the cat who took first prize at the bird show? He ate the prize-winning budgie.

HAM: I've just had to shoot one of the dogs!
MRS NOAH: Was it mad?
HAM: Let's say it wasn't too pleased . . .

JAPHETH: I love my dog, but there's one thing I can't stand about him.
HAM: What's that?
JAPHETH: When there's a storm he always lies under my bed.
HAM: That's because he's frightened. There's nothing wrong with that.
JAPHETH: But he doesn't leave any room for me!

NOAH: And what do you call this scruffy little mongrel?
JAPHETH: Sandwich — cos he's half-bred.

What paper do cats read on Sundays?
The Mews of the World.

What do you get if you cross a gun dog and a telephone?
A golden receiver.

NOAH: A black and white cat crossed my path this morning.
MRS NOAH: And what happened?
NOAH: Since then my luck's been patchy.

NOAH: That star up there is the Dog Star.
HAM: You can't be Sirius!

MRS NOAH: Where have you been?
NOAH: I took the cat fishing.
MRS NOAH: And did you catch anything?
NOAH: No. I think next time I'll use a maggot.

When should a mouse carry an umbrella?
When it's raining cats and dogs.

JAPHETH: Did you hear that the cat won a milk-drinking contest?
MRS NOAH: It did well, did it?
JAPHETH: Yes, it won by six laps.

Why are cats bigger at night than in the morning?
Because at night they're let out and in the morning they're taken in again.

SHEM: What's this dog called?
JAPHETH: Isaiah.
SHEM: Why is that?
JAPHETH: Because one eye's higher than the other.

Why did the dog refuse to go into the Ark?
Doggone if Noah knows.

NOAH: I feed this dog garlic sandwiches every day.
SHEM: Why?
NOAH: So that his bark's worse than his bite.

What happened when the cat swallowed ten pence?
There was money in the kitty.

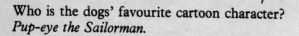

MRS NOAH: Keep that dog out of the cabin — it's got fleas.
NOAH: Stay out of the cabin, Doggie — it's full of fleas.

How is cat food usually sold?
Purr can.

Who is the dogs' favourite cartoon character?
Pup-eye the Sailorman.

JAPHETH: Help! Help! A dog just bit my leg!
MRS NOAH: Did you put anything on it?
JAPHETH: No, it seemed to like it just as it was.

JAPHETH: You know, this dog is just like one of the family.
NOAH: Which one of us did you have in mind?

HAM: Can a dalmatian change its spots?
NOAH: Of course it can. It can get up and move to another spot whenever it feels like it.

Why is a kitten sitting on the fence like a pound coin?
Because it has a head on one side and a tail on the other.

NOAH: Is this dog a pointer or a setter?
MRS NOAH: Neither — it's a disappointer and an upsetter.

HAM: Have you ever seen a catfish?
NOAH: Yes.
HAM: How did it manage to hold the rod?

Mrs Noah and Shem were sitting in the cabin one rainy afternoon. On Mrs Noah's lap sat one of the Ark's cats. "Meow," said the cat.

"I don't like that animal," said Shem. "It keeps making catty remarks."

What goes tick-tock, tick-tock — woof, woof, woof?
A watchdog.

NOAH: I don't think you're ever going to get that dog to do tricks. It's too disobedient.
MRS NOAH: Don't you believe it — do you remember how disobedient you were when we first married?

What did the cat do after he'd swallowed a piece of cheese?
He sat by the mousehole and waited with baited breath.

What's the most dangerous dog in the world?
A chihuahua with a machine gun.

Which cat causes chaos wherever it goes?
Cat-astrophe.

MRS NOAH: This dog's nice, but his legs are rather short.
JAPHETH: What are you complaining about? His legs reach all the way down to the ground.

NOAH: I think I'll teach this dog some tricks.
SHEM: There are a few things you should know before you start.
NOAH: What's that?
SHEM: More than the dog . . .

NOAH: What sort of dog is that?
HAM: A police dog.
NOAH: It doesn't look like a police dog to me.
HAM: That's because it's an undercover agent.

What do you call a dog who likes to have a wash three times a day?
A shampoodle.

JAPHETH: This cat wants to join the Red Cross.
NOAH: Why does it want to do that?
JAPHETH: Because it wants to be a First Aid Kit.

JAPHETH: Eight cats were in a lifeboat and one of them jumped over the side. How many were left?

MRS NOAH: Seven, of course.

JAPHETH: No — none, because they were all copy-cats.

What did the dog say when he sat on a piece of sandpaper?

"Ruff!"

MRS NOAH: What's this dog's name?

HAM: Ginger.

MRS NOAH: Why do you call him Ginger?

HAM: Because he snaps.

Why do cats and dogs turn round and round in circles before they go to sleep?

Because one good turn deserves another.

NOAH: This dog has no tail.

MRS NOAH: How can you tell when it's happy?

NOAH: When it's happy it stops biting me.

HAM: There's a black cat sitting on the kitchen table.

MRS NOAH: Don't worry — black cats are lucky.

HAM: Well this one certainly is — he just ate our dinner!

NOAH: Why do you call your dog Blacksmith?

SHEM: Because every time someone comes in he makes a bolt for the door.

If ten dogs chase two cats, what's the time?
Ten after two.

MRS NOAH: This cat never stops purring.
JAPHETH: That's because it's a Purrsian cat.

Now you see it, now you don't. What is it?
A white cat walking over a zebra crossing.

What's the difference between Japheth and his dog when they go out together for a walk?
Japheth wears trousers and the dog pants.

Why is a vicious dog a starving man's best friend?
Because he's certain to give him a bite.

ALL ABOARD THE ARK!

What's a polygon?
A parrot that's flown away.

NOAH: Did you hear about the man who was trampled on when a flock of sheep stampeded?
SHEM: No, what happened?
NOAH: He was dyed-in-the-wool.

What do you call a mad octopus?
A crazy mixed-up squid.

SHEM: The Egyptian worm's got a terrible cold.
MRS NOAH: Who did he catch it from?
SHEM: His mummy.

What's the difference between a wallaby and a woodcutter?
One hops and chews, the other chops and hews.

What looks like a hippopotamus and flies?
A flying hippopotamus.

HAM: What kind of car do sausage dogs like driving?
NOAH: I don't know.
HAM: A Rolls.

What did the little mouse say when he saw a bat?
"Look at that angel!"

NOAH: Help! The monkeys are throwing coconuts at each other.
MRS NOAH: It's gorilla warfare!

NOAH: Where does that polar bear come from?
JAPHETH: Alaska.
NOAH: Don't bother, I'll ask her myself.

JAPHETH: This dog is so lazy that I have to wag his tail for him.
SHEM: That's nothing — this one is so lazy that he fetches yesterday's paper.

What do lady sheep call their woolly coats?
Ewe-niforms.

SHEM: Someone has stolen our dogs!
MRS NOAH: Call the police.
SHEM: I have, but they say they haven't a lead to go on.

Where do you go to weigh a whale?
To a whale weigh station.

Why is a peacock like the number nine?
Because without its tail it would be nothing.

MRS NOAH: This chicken is sick.
JAPHETH: What's wrong with it?
MRS NOAH: It's got people-pox.

What's brown, has four legs and a trunk?
A mouse returning from holiday.

NOAH: Can all the birds vote in the election?
JAPHETH: All of them except the mynah bird
— he's too young.

JAPHETH: Shem has just crossed an elephant
with a mole.
NOAH: The idiot!
JAPHETH: I know — just think of those huge
holes all over the garden!

SHEM: What's the strongest animal in the
world?
MRS NOAH: The elephant?
SHEM: No — the snail, because it carries its
house on its back.

SHEM: What do you get when you cross an elephant with a Boy Scout?
JAPHETH: No idea.
SHEM: An elephant that helps old ladies across the road.

Why do storks stand on only one leg?
Because if they lifted the other one, they'd fall over.

NOAH: Why do elephants have trunks?
MRS NOAH: I don't know.
NOAH: So that when a mouse frightens them they have somewhere to hide.

NOAH: This parrot comes from Edinburgh.
JAPHETH: What's its name?
NOAH: Mac-aw.

What is the crocodiles' favourite card game?
Snap.

Which animal is the best at adding up?
An octoplus.

SHEM: What animal lives in an abbey?
NOAH: A chipmunk.

What do you call a snake who wears a bowler hat and carries an umbrella?
A civil serpent.

MRS NOAH: Why is that elephant painting her toenails yellow, red, brown and green?
NOAH: So she can hide in a tube of Smarties.

HAM: Why are your feet so flat?
JAPHETH: I tried to teach an elephant to dance.

Why wasn't the rocking-horse allowed on the Ark?
Because it was a phony pony.

JAPHETH: It's time to put fresh water in the fish tank.
MRS NOAH: But the fish haven't drunk it all yet!

MRS NOAH: Sometimes it gets so difficult telling all these cats apart!
JAPHETH: What you need is a catalogue . . .

NOAH: That monkey is absolutely stupid!
JAPHETH: That chimpanzee over there?
NOAH: More like a chumpanzee.

Why was the sheep arrested?
Because it made a ewe-turn on the motorway.

MRS NOAH: You musn't shout at the cat like that.
SHEM: Why not?
MRS NOAH: Because you'll hurt her felines.

What's pigskin for?
Holding a pig together.

SHEM: Help! Mum's fallen over the side!
SHEM: And there's a shark in the water!
JAPHETH: Don't panic — it's a *man*-eating shark.

JAPHETH: Have you heard the Ark orchestra? The cats play the violins.
NOAH: And what do the mice play?
JAPHETH: Mouse organs.

MRS NOAH: Which kind of bird has a shell?
NOAH: The turtledove.

Where do chickens live in New York?
The Henpire States Building.

NOAH: Why do bees fly through the air with their back legs crossed?
MRS NOAH: I give up.
NOAH: Because they're looking for a BP station!

Why can't the leopard escape from the Ark?
Every time he tries, he's spotted.

What do camels carry in the rain?
Humpbrellas.

NOAH: Come and help me look for the gerbil with one eye.
JAPHETH: Wouldn't it be easier if I used both eyes?

What is a myth?
A lady moth who hasn't got married.

MRS NOAH: We really must get that hedgehog some glasses.
NOAH: Why should we do that?
MRS NOAH: The poor thing's just got engaged to a scrubbing brush!

SHEM: I've just crossed a chicken and a bell.
JAPHETH: And what did you get?
SHEM: An alarm cluck.

HAM: Mum — I keep thinking I'm a bird.
MRS NOAH: Go straight to bed, and I'll come and tweet you in a minute.

When is the vet busiest?
When it's raining cats and dogs.

Have you heard the story of Algy and the Bear?
It's a short story and it goes like this:
    Algy met a bear.
    The bear was bulgy.
    The bulge was Algy.

NOAH: Those sheep have a nice tan.
MRS NOAH: That's because they're just back from holiday.
NOAH: Where did they go?
MRS NOAH: The Baa-haaa-maaas.

What do you get if you cross a frog and a kilt?
Hopscotch.

SHEM: I've just crossed a rabbit with a leek.
MRS NOAH: And what have you got?
SHEM: Bunions!

JAPHETH: The hares have escaped!
SHEM: Quick! Comb the area!

Where do fish wash their fins?
In the river basin.

What happened when the grizzly bear ate Russ
Abbott?
He felt funny.

NOAH: What do you get if you cross a pig and a
telephone wire?
HAM: No idea.
NOAH: Crackling on the line.

SHEM: When does a yard have four feet?
JAPHETH: Don't be stupid, a yard only has
three feet.
SHEM: Not when there's a dog in it!

What always carries hundreds of needles but can't sew?
A porcupine.

NOAH: Have you ever gone hunting bear?
HAM: No, but I once went swimming bare!

What happened when the frog's car broke down?
It was toad away.

MRS NOAH: Why is that elephant lying in the middle of the path?
JAPHETH: He's trying to trip the ants over.

NOAH: You need to know more about the chickens.
MRS NOAH: How do I find out?
NOAH: In the Hencyclopaedia.

Which animal is it best to be with in a snowstorm?
A little otter.

SHEM: Look at this little newt.
JAPHETH: What do you call it?
SHEM: Tiny — because it's my newt (minute).

Why did the pig squeal?
Because he saw the barn dance.

JAPHETH: How can you tell the difference between a stoat and a weasel?
NOAH: I don't know.
JAPHETH: Well, a weasel's a weasel, but a stoat's stoatally different.

MRS NOAH: That owl has a terrible memory.
SHEM: Why do you say that?
MRS NOAH: I've told it my name a dozen times, yet each time I go by it says "Who who who?"

What do geese get when they're freezing?
Goose pimples.

SHEM: What are you cooking the frogs for dinner tonight?
MRS NOAH: Potatoes.
SHEM: Chips?
MRS NOAH: No, croakettes.

SHEM: I call mosquitoes arithmetic bugs.

NOAH: Why?

SHEM: Because they add to our misery, subtract from our pleasure and multiply quickly.

What's the difference between a dog and a sheep?

One carries fleas and the other carries fleece.

NOAH: Which dog is the most expensive to buy?

JAPHETH: I don't know.

NOAH: A deerhound.

NOAH: That chicken is a champion boxer.

JAPHETH: Is it really?

NOAH: Yes, it's featherweight champion of the world.

Why aren't there any aspirins in the desert?

Because the paracetamol (the parrots eat them all).

Where do fish go when they're short of money?
The prawn broker.

Why did the blackbird keep going to the library?
He was looking for bookworms.

JAPHETH: Why does that dog turn round and round in circles before it goes to sleep?
NOAH: Because it's a watchdog and it has to wind itself up.

Why do bats suck mints?
Because they're worried about bat breath.

NOAH: What's even worse than a centipede with bunions?
MRS NOAH: I've no idea.
NOAH: A crocodile with toothache!

What do you get if you cross a cow with a tortoise?
Longlife milk.

SHEM: Did you know that it takes four sheep to make a jumper?

JAPHETH: I didn't even know sheep could knit.

Which sort of birds come from Portugal?
Portu-geese.

HAM: I'm going to prove that a horse has six legs.

JAPHETH: Don't be ridiculous — horses have only four legs.

HAM: That's where you're wrong. They have forelegs in front and two legs behind . . .

What goes stomp, stomp, stomp, stomp?
An elephant in a terrible huff.

SHEM: What's the difference between a gymnast and a duck?

JAPHETH: I don't know.

SHEM: One goes quick on her legs and one goes quack on her legs.

Which animal likes skin-diving?
A gnat.

JAPHETH: Which bird doesn't build its own nest?
HAM: A cuckoo.
JAPHETH: Why do you say that?
HAM: Everyone knows that cuckoos live in clocks!

NOAH: Do you remember the name of the man who put his arm down the lion's throat?
SHEM: I think they call him Lefty now.

When are dogs banned from going on buses?
At the peke period.

NOAH: There's going to be a terrible storm tonight.
SHEM: How do you know?
NOAH: I can hear the elephants' ears flapping in the wind.

What did the budgie think when the cat grabbed it by the tail?
"That's the end of me!"

HAM: Those rabbits must be brilliant at arithmetic.
NOAH: Why do you say that?
HAM: Well, they multiply so quickly.

What did the spider say when she made a hole in her web?
Darn it!

What's pink and zooms around in the sea at three hundred miles an hour?
A jet-propelled lobster.

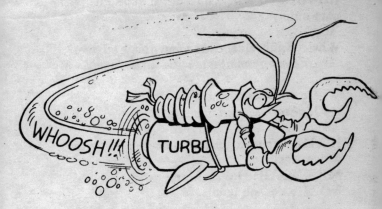

SHEM: Isn't it wonderful the way little chicks get out of their shells?
HAM: What amazes me is how they got in there in the first place!

Who is the bees' favourite pop star?
Sting.

JAPHETH: What do you call that horse over there? The one with the number on its bottom.
NOAH: Reg.

Why did the monkey scratch himself?
Because he was the only one who knew where it itched.

MRS NOAH: What song do the lions sing at Christmas?
JAPHETH: Jungle bells, jungle bells.

JAPHETH: What's the difference between a fake five-pound note and a crazy rabbit?
NOAH: I give up.
JAPHETH: One's bad money and the other's a mad bunny.

Why do squirrels spend so much time up trees?
To get away from all the nuts on the ground.

Where do birds invest their money?
On the Stork Market.

NOAH: That hedgehog has been fighting the wolves again.
MRS NOAH: Did he win?
NOAH: Yes, on points.

What do you call a male cow taking an afternoon nap?
A bulldozer.

Why did the bald man put a
rabbit on his head?
Because he wanted a head of hare.

NOAH: That horse is terribly bossy.
JAPHETH: Yes, she's a real old nag.

What did one bee say to the other bee?
"Buzz off!"

SHEM: We're having fish for pudding.
NOAH: Fish for *pudding*?
SHEM: Yes, jellyfish.

MRS NOAH: Those wolves are just like
playing cards.
NOAH: Why is that?
MRS NOAH: Because they come in packs.

If a mother whale had a boy and a girl whale,
what would they be called?
Blubber and sister.

One of the lions had escaped from its cage on
the Ark and Japheth and Shem went to look for
it. Eventually they found its tracks on the
middle deck. "Okay," said Japheth, "you see
where they go to and I'll see where they came
from . . .

JAPHETH: What's that bee doing?
HAM: Painting a portrait.
JAPHETH: So that's Pablo Bee-casso, the
famous artist!

What's the difference between a skunk and a chipmunk?
The skunk doesn't use deodorant.

SHEM: I read in a book that man is descended from the monkeys.
NOAH: That's what the scientists say, son.
SHEM: But what about those monkeys that are still monkeys?
NOAH: Well, they're the smart ones!

What's the difference between a bored audience and a sick cow?
The cow moos and the audience boos.

Which ant sorts out all the Ark's finances?
The account-ant.

Who's the bees' favourite composer?
Bee-thoven.

SHEM: The robin and the sparrow are going to get married.
MRS NOAH: How sweet! Was it love at first sight?
SHEM: No, he egged her on a bit.

Which fish always goes to heaven when it dies?
The angel fish.

NOAH: What's the name of the panic you feel when you're surrounded by sharks?
MRS NOAH: Jawstrophobia.

What did the idiot call his pet tiger?
Spot.

SHEM: What's worse than being with a fool?
HAM: Fooling with a bee!

Why were the elephants the last animals to leave the Ark?
Because they had to pack their trunks.

JAPHETH: How would you define a slug?
NOAH: A homeless snail.

Which reptile is best at maths?
An adder.

MRS NOAH: Why are all the animals laughing?
HAM: One of the owls just told a joke.
MRS NOAH: He's a real hoot!

What does every duckling become when it first
learns to swim?
Wet.

What fur do you get from skunks?
As fur as you can.

What did Paddington, SuperTed and Winnie
the Pooh take on holiday?
The bear essentials.

NOAH: Those goats are so easy to fool!
MRS NOAH: Why's that?
NOAH: They'll swallow anything.

What is a panther?
Someone who makes panths.

JAPHETH: Have you ever had toad-in-the-
hole?
NOAH: No, but I've had a frog in my throat.

MRS NOAH: What are all those insects doing?
SHEM: They're listening to the radio.
MRS NOAH: The Bee Bee Cee?

Why is a wild horse like an egg?
Because they both have to be broken.

SHEM: Shall we let the turkey join our pop group?
HAM: We'll have to — he's the only one with drumsticks.

What happens to a badger after it's one year old?
It becomes two years old.

MRS NOAH: Who's the cat who walks around wearing a leather jacket and chains?
HAM: That's the Punk Panther.

NOAH: These fish are terribly polite.
JAPHETH: It's because they go around in schools.

What are apricots?
They're places where baby monkeys sleep.

NOAH: Which Christmas pantomime is about a cat in a chemist's shop?
MRS NOAH: I don't know.
NOAH: Puss in Boots!

Where do cats invest their money?
In the Tabby National.

SHEM: I went for a walk in a field one day and found myself surrounded by lions.
JAPHETH: Were you scared?
SHEM: No — they were dandelions.

What's the difference between a vicious alsatian and a hot dog?
One bites the hand that feeds it, the other feeds the hand that bites it.

NOAH: What have you got there?
MRS NOAH: A wombat.
NOAH: What are we supposed to do with it?
MRS NOAH: Play wom?

SHEM: Have you got an aspirin?
MRS NOAH: Why, do you need one?
SHEM: The skunk's got a stinking headache.

What did Mrs Firefly say to Mrs Bluebottle?
"My son is such a bright boy!"

When is a kangaroo like water?
When it springs.

SHEM: Dad, do caterpillars taste good?
NOAH: Be quiet, I'm trying to eat my lunch. (Later) . . . Now, what was that you were saying about caterpillars?
SHEM: Nothing — it's just that there was a big one on your lettuce. But it's gone now.

Which part of a fish weighs the most?
The scales.

If your best friend owned a peacock which came and laid an egg in your garden, to whom would the egg belong — you or your friend?
Neither – because peahens, not peacocks, lay eggs.

NOAH: Why has that wolf got wooden legs?
JAPHETH: Because it's a timber wolf.

NOAH: What's the best way of stopping a parrot from falling off its perch?
SHEM: I don't know.
NOAH: Use Polly-grip.

Why did the hedgehog cross the road?
To see his flat mate.

JAPHETH: Can I have the nutcrackers, please?
MRS NOAH: What do you want them for?
JAPHETH: For the toothless squirrel.

MRS NOAH: This baby goat has terrible table manners.
NOAH: Well, he's only a kid.

Why didn't the piglets listen to their father?
Because he was an old boar.

NOAH: The frogs are at it again!
MRS NOAH: What are they doing?
NOAH: They're making beer.
MRS NOAH: But how do they do that?
NOAH: They start with some hops . . .

Which famous fish only comes out to swim at night?
A starfish.

JAPHETH: Have you noticed how all the animals come up and lick my hand?

MRS NOAH: They wouldn't be so friendly if you ate with a knife and fork.

NOAH: When I was in bed last night a ghostly insect came and haunted me.

SHEM: How terrible. What was it?

NOAH: A zom-bee.

JAPHETH: It was incredible — there was a lion in front of me and a tiger behind, and next to me was an elephant . . .

NOAH: And then what happened?

JAPHETH: The roundabout stopped and I had to get off.

What is the definition of impeccable?
Something the hens can't eat.

NOAH: Which duck would you like for a pet — this duck or that duck?

SHEM: Eider would do.

MRS NOAH: Why is the letter T so important to a stick insect?

JAPHETH: I don't know.

MRS NOAH: Because without it, it would be a sick insect.

What's the best way to prevent a skunk smelling?
Put a clothes-peg on its nose.

201

CROSSBREEDS

While they've been at sea, Noah and his family have had the chance to try crossing some of their animals — with hilarious results!

What do you get if you cross a hen and a banjo?
A chicken that plucks itself.

MRS NOAH: I'm going to cross a turkey and an octopus.
NOAH: Why?
MRS NOAH: So that everyone can have a leg with their Christmas dinner.

What do you get if you cross a red cat and a blue parrot?
A purple carrot.

NOAH: I'm going to cross an elephant with an abominable snowman.
JAPHETH: And what will you get?
NOAH: A jumbo yeti.

MRS NOAH: I'm going to cross a kangaroo and a mink.
NOAH: But why?
MRS NOAH: I want a fur coat with pockets.

What would you get if you crossed a zebra with a pig?
Striped sausages.

What happened when Noah crossed a small dog with a vegetable?
He got a Jack Brussell terrier.

NOAH: I've crossed a hedgehog with a mole.
MRS NOAH: And what did you get?
NOAH: A leaky tunnel.

What happened when Noah crossed a hen with a waitress?
He got a chicken that lays tables.

JAPHETH: I've just crossed a hyena with a lion.
SHEM: And what did you get?
JAPHETH: I'm not sure, but when it laughs we'd better join in!

What do you get if you cross a bee with a bell?
A humdinger.

NOAH: I'm going to cross a flying insect and a camel.
MRS NOAH: And what will you get?
NOAH: A hump-backed midge.

What do you get if you cross a parrot and an elephant?
Something that tells everything it remembers.

JAPHETH: I wish I hadn't crossed that yak with the parrot.
HAM: Why not?
JAPHETH: Because I got a yackety-yak!

What do you get if you cross a cow and a camel?
Lumpy milkshakes.

SHEM: I've just crossed a crocodile with a lettuce.
NOAH: And what did you get?
SHEM: A green salad that snaps.

What happens when you cross a flea with a pig?
You get pork scratchings.

What do you get if you cross a billy goat and a male pig?
A crashing bore.

NOAH: I think I'll cross a duck and a whale.
JAPHETH: What will you get?
NOAH: Moby Duck.

What do you get if you cross a male cat and a canary?
A peeping tom.

SHEM: I wonder what I'd get if I crossed a tiger with an ape man?
MRS NOAH: Tarzan stripes for ever?

What do you get if you cross a squirrel and a kangaroo?
An animal that always carries nuts in its pocket.

What do you get if you cross a four-wheel drive vehicle and a dog?
A Land Rover.

SHEM: I think I'll cross an elephant and a pig.
HAM: And what do you expect to get?
SHEM: Huge rashers of bacon.

What happened when Noah crossed a hyena with the North Sea?
He got waves of laughter.

SHEM: I've crossed a chicken with a harp.
NOAH: And what have you got?
SHEM: A chicken that plays a tune when it's plucked.

JAPHETH: I'm going to cross a porcupine with a worm.
NOAH: And what will you get?
JAPHETH: Barbed wire.

What do you get if you cross a sheep-dog and a dish of jelly?
The collie-wobbles.

NOAH: What happens if you cross a gorilla with a footballer?
MRS NOAH: I don't know.
NOAH: Neither do I, but if it tried to score a goal I wouldn't try to stop it!

NOAH: I wonder what we'd get if we crossed a lion with a mouse?
MRS NOAH: Mighty Mouse!

What do you get if you cross an elephant with a goldfish?
Swimming trunks.

What do you get if you cross an electric eel with a pelican?
A huge electric bill.

MRS NOAH: I've crossed a poodle with a chicken.
HAM: And what did you get?
MRS NOAH: Pooched eggs.

What do you get if you cross Concorde with a kangaroo?
A plane that makes short hops.

JAPHETH: I've crossed a rat with a woodpecker.
SHEM: And what did you get?
JAPHETH: A rat-a-tat-tat.

What do you get if you cross an owl with a skunk?
A bird that smells but doesn't give a hoot.

HAM: I wonder what you get if you cross a sheep and an octopus?
JAPHETH: A sweater with eight sleeves?

What do you get if you cross a cement mixer with a hen?
A bricklayer.